SELL NOW!

Also by John R. Talbott

*The Coming Crash in the Housing Market: 10 Things You Can
Do Now to Protect Your Most Valuable Investment*

*Where America Went Wrong:
And How to Regain Her Democratic Ideals*

SELL NOW!

The End of the Housing Bubble

John R. Talbott

St. Martin's Griffin
New York

www.stmartins.com

Library of Congress Cataloging-in-Publication Data

ISBN 0-312-35788-5
EAN 978-0-312-35788-7

First Edition: January 2006

10 9 8 7 6 5 4 3 2 1

Contents

Author's Note

It is common to write nonfiction in a passive, unemotional, almost detached voice so as to appear completely objective and rational.

In writing this book, I took a different approach. At times, I allowed my anger and bitterness to enter my writing style. I decided that these emotions were a very real part of the story that I tell here. By including these emotions in the narrative, I try to bring the reader closer to the underlying truths in this tale.

Logic and emotion both have important parts to play in conveying the truth. The reader would be suspicious if I told such a tale of deceit, greed, self-indulgence, government neglect and corruption, and industry-wide collusion and ineptitude without expressing any emotions.

The fact that many average homeowners and their families will suffer greatly for years to come correcting the wrongs presented here is only further reason for my anger. If I can turn my anger into your taking positive action to change the system, then the entire effort will have been more than worthwhile.

I hope you benefit from what I believe is a new and creative analysis of what our homes are really worth, who has the most to fear as home prices begin to trade down, and why it is so important we act now to return rationality to our housing and mortgage markets.

—John R. Talbott
johntalbs@gmail.com

Introduction

In 2003, I wrote a book entitled *The Coming Crash in the Housing Market*. At the time, I was one of only a handful of people who expressed concern about the direction real housing prices had been heading in for decades. Today, you can't turn on the television without someone using the word "bubble." (Nationally, home values, after adjusting for general inflation, had increased almost 61 percent from 1981 to 2003, and now have increased an additional 35 percent from their 2003 levels in just the last three years.) I was concerned about the unusually high prices being paid for homes relative to rents and household incomes, and I also raised questions about the health of the entire housing and mortgage industries. How could I know that things would have to get much worse before they could get better?

I reserved most of my wrath for Fannie Mae and Freddie Mac, which I viewed as overly leveraged with debt and poorly managed bureaucracies due for a fall. (The month *The Coming Crash* was published, Freddie Mac announced it needed to restate some $5 billion of earnings, followed quickly by Fannie Mae's announcement that it needed to restate their earnings by some $11 billion cumulatively. Both slowed their aggressive asset expansion and both replaced senior executives in management shake-ups.)

While many viewed the housing and mortgage industries as stable, well-run businesses, I found them incredibly incestuous. The problem was that they pretended to be operating in a free market when nothing of the sort existed. Most of us take great comfort in the belief that market-determined prices are usually right because they are based on voluntary exchanges and are backed by real money, not just people's opinions about value.

I argued that the housing market was not an ideal free market. The home acquisitions were so large, and the homebuyers contributed so little of the financing, that the real decision maker on how much to pay for a house appeared to be the bank and, ultimately, Fannie Mae or Freddie Mac, the institutions that ended up holding most of the paper. It was bad enough that individual homebuyers were not sensitive to possibly paying too much for a home since it was not their money at risk. It was even worse to find that Fannie and Freddie were rather indifferent because they held the ultimate trump card—an implied guarantee on the credit quality of their debt supplied by you, the American taxpayer.

Part of the reason I am writing this new book is that I don't think the message of the first book was completely absorbed. But the major reason for this new effort is that the world has changed a great deal in the last three years. There is a vast amount of new evidence that needs explaining. Many pundits have weighed in with superficial explanations of the housing boom that need correcting. There is also new academic research that requires interpreting. This book is a completely new and fresh look at the housing problem, and I believe the reader will find it very convincing in its argument that troubled times are ahead. In the first book, I argued that the housing boom was national, now we will see it is global.

No one can predict with absolute certainty what the future holds. But if I told you that there was a 50 percent chance that real housing prices would drop by 30 percent or more in many of the major cities of the world, what action would you take? I will grant you that home prices may have a 35 percent chance of staying at these relatively high levels, and even a 15 percent chance of heading still higher in the short run. But what would you do to protect your family and your home investment if I was right about the probability of a major decline in price? If I told you there was a 50 percent chance of your getting run over if you ran across a busy highway, you wouldn't try it just because I wasn't "certain" of an accident. Similarly, all indications are that we are in for a fairly rough ride in the housing market for the next five to seven years, and it only makes sense for you to plan accordingly.

When prices are up and times are good, it is quite incredible how our optimism allows us to play with our accumulated profits in a home or stock position. At a casino, it is always easier to gamble with the house's money, and difficult to stop when you're ahead. But a good investor is one who examines all possible future outcomes, and acts to protect his wealth before calamity strikes.

Say you purchased a home in 1981 for $150,000. Today, the market value of that property might be between $450,000 and $1,200,000, depending on where you live. Now, if I am right, you run the very real risk of losing anywhere from $200,000 to $500,000 in real value as housing prices trend downward over the next five years. What are you going to do?

If you are like most Americans, you probably will do nothing. The reasons include not believing that a housing market that has increased for forty straight years could ever go down, not wanting to miss additional profits if it continues going up, or not wanting to hassle with moving into a rental or smaller home on a temporary basis.

If you are trying to accumulate wealth in your lifetime, you are missing a once-in-a-lifetime opportunity. By remaining in your home and doing nothing, you are creating paper profits, and we all know they have zero value. Profits are not real until you realize them by cashing out. If you don't cash out now, you are missing the opportunity to create real wealth of between $200,000 and $500,000.

This may not sound like much in a world where housing prices are increasing $100,000 a year. But imagine the new world after housing prices collapse. Not only is housing going to head south, but it will take the economy with it. There are not going to be any opportunities to earn 15 to 20 percent on your money. If you can earn a positive real return at all, say 2 percent per year after inflation, you will be doing very well. So to replicate the $200,000 to $500,000 windfall you missed by not selling your home at the peak, you will have to patiently wait twenty to sixty years or more as your savings accrue at a modest 2 to 3 percent a year. What you are passing up is the opportunity to create a lifetime of savings in one fell swoop. And when prices decline and the economy becomes troubled, cash will be king. People who have monetized their paper profits by selling at the peak will have real cash with which to make even more profitable investments. Picture yourself as one of only a few people at a bank auction of foreclosed real estate who has actual cash to spend on inexpensive properties after the crash.

Because your home is probably the largest acquisition you will ever make, and because home prices have escalated so dramatically, you are being given a once-in-a-lifetime opportunity to be really wealthy for a change. But you must act. You must sell. It will be easier for those who own multiple investment properties to make the decision to sell since that is what investors do when prices are expected to decline. Vacation homes should also be sold—they can always be bought back later at a lower price. But for those who only own one home, it is a much tougher decision. Transaction costs are high and families do become awfully attached to their homes. It is just a question of whether you want to get rich today and avoid the hassles of a crash in prices in the future, or would rather sit tight and try to weather the storm. For some, doing nothing will turn out to be a high-stakes gamble in which they will face the very real possibility of losing their homes to foreclosure.

But before you can make such an important decision, you need to know that today's high housing prices are an abnormal bubble about to burst, and to understand all the forces that have driven housing prices so far so fast. Armed with the information in this book, you'll be prepared to make the right decision at the right time, for the right reasons.

A number of different circumstances have to happen for home prices to appreciate. Somehow, we have had all of them present for a very long time. But that is no guarantee these forces will align properly in the future.

First, people must really see great value in their homes or they would not agree to pay such high prices. At these price levels, home-buyers are often forgoing many other investment and consumption alternatives because the monthly mortgage payment commands such a large percentage of their disposable income. What is it that motivates people to pay one, two, or three million dollars for a house? I answer that question in chapter 9, but for now let's say that the reason is as old as mankind. And no, it isn't just greed that is driving us.

Because homes represent such large purchases for the typical homebuyer, a second important element that must be in place before prices can increase is adequate financing. Regardless of how much you may want to buy a particular home, in most cases there will be no sale unless you can convince a bank to lend you the needed funds. In today's upside-down world, it is typically the bank that is convincing you to spend the extra money. But, regardless, for homes to increase in price, somebody must be willing to extend greater and greater amounts of financing.

The banks never think this completely through. Four years ago they may have been willing to grant a mortgage with only 10 percent down. But if they do a similar 10 percent down deal today, after home prices have risen 40 percent in real terms, they are actually making the loan at 130 percent of the market value four years ago. Would it have been reasonable, four years ago, for a bank to extend a loan equal to 130 percent of the market value of a home? If not, why is it reasonable today? One answer is that the market price has changed. But what if that change is not guaranteed to be permanent? Would you lend somebody a million dollars on a home that was worth only $785,000 four years ago? We will see that the banks' willingness to extend mortgage moneys on very aggressive terms is a prime reason we are in the mess we are today.

A third requirement of ever-increasing home prices is that many current homeowners must be reluctant to sell at today's prices. What do you think will happen to home prices if current homeowners suddenly become convinced that prices have peaked and are heading south? Without a single newly constructed house coming on the market, the supply of willing sellers would increase so dramatically that the number of houses offered for sale on the market would quickly dwarf any pent-up or excess demand.

A fourth element should be in place for real estate to appreciate in price. There should not be an opportunity to add a substantial supply of newly constructed homes at a lower price than the market. New homes can cost anywhere from $60,000 to $300,000 to build, just in construction costs, so there must be some reason why average home prices are so much higher than these replacement values. One possible explanation is that new home construction is being artificially constrained by strict zoning limits and building restrictions in many communities across the country. I will argue that this is not the primary reason prices have increased the fastest in the most desirable communities of our country.

The other reason that homes might sell for more than construction costs is that the value of the underlying land has increased significantly. I will provide very strong evidence that this is exactly what has happened in our most exclusive neighborhoods. These increases in land value aren't necessarily permanent or based on economic fundamentals, but communities with the least raw land available for residential development have enjoyed the greatest price appreciation in their homes.

There is always the argument that home prices can increase solely because of the irrationality and stupidity of the buyers. I shy away from this catchall excuse because it is often offered for any poorly understood change in economic circumstances. If no one has developed a rational explanation for why prices have increased, it is always easy to just blame the buyers for overpaying. While attractive for its completeness, such an explanation should be frowned upon for its universal appeal, its ease of application, and its failure to further our understanding of how markets actually operate.

One step short of blaming completely blithering idiotic overpaying buyers is an explanation of human behavior that suggests that we can find ourselves caught up in Ponzi-like schemes in which early investors are rewarded and later investors are punished. We shall see that residential real estate, for a number of reasons, fits very well into a traditional Ponzi-like model of pyramiding profits until the game runs out. Who doesn't know someone who rolled their profits from one house into a much bigger bet on a larger home? And which of us is not affected personally when we hear neighbors brag about the hundreds of thousands in profits they have realized in their home buying? These are the very real examples of the short-term profit potential of many Ponzi schemes that make rational thought and action difficult.

In order to understand the stability of the housing market we must understand all of these required elements of an appreciating market. It is incredible that all the elements have been in place so long and the market has appreciated so consistently year to year. The odds that the sun and the moon and the stars will stay perfectly aligned in the future are tiny.

The *Economist* magazine calls the current housing boom "the biggest bubble in history," with world residential real estate value having appreciated from some $40 trillion to over $70 trillion over the last decade. You might justifiably ask how such a bubble would be allowed to propagate unless it were real. Our government officials and regulators should be actively warning us if there were any real danger. I explain in chapter 4 that the allegiance of our elected representatives may have changed over time so that they no longer think of their primary task as protecting or serving the American public.

In chapter 10, I try to paint a picture of what might happen if home prices begin to decline. There is no dead man's brake to automatically slow or stop the process once it starts. It becomes self-generating. Small declines in home prices encourage greater sales, and fewer buyers, and lower prices, and more foreclosures, and a weaker economy, and more job losses, and a weaker banking system, and more home sales, and more pain for everyone involved. Just as in 2001 when NASDAQ investors gave back almost all of their gains of the previous decade once their Internet stocks crashed, so, too, will most homeowners give back almost all of the paper profits they have temporarily garnered during this real estate boom. Unfortunately, the economy and banking system will be so permanently damaged that Americans will be much worse off for years to come for having ever played this very dangerous game with bubbling and booming real estate.

SELL NOW!

1

Can We Predict Home Prices?

Housing prices in America have been increasing for fifty straight years. This appreciation has accelerated over the last eleven years, and the average home has nearly doubled in price. And as we shall examine in more detail in chapter 3, home prices in our biggest cities have been growing even faster. Many of our largest cities have seen their average homes triple in price over the last eleven years.

What can we infer from this information? Because prices have increased in the past, are they expected to increase further in the future? Is there some underlying force that is constantly driving home prices ever higher? And, if so, should we expect prices to continue to increase as they have recently? Let's look at some data and see if we can make any reasonable deductions.

As can be seen in Figure 1.1, price increases in this market have been dramatic. Average home prices have doubled historically, and the six largest cities have witnessed a tripling in prices. Can we make a prediction of where prices are headed in this market by examining this recent trend? One obvious approach is to continue the trend line along its recent trajectory and assume this will continue for the

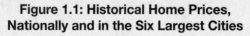

**Figure 1.1: Historical Home Prices,
Nationally and in the Six Largest Cities**

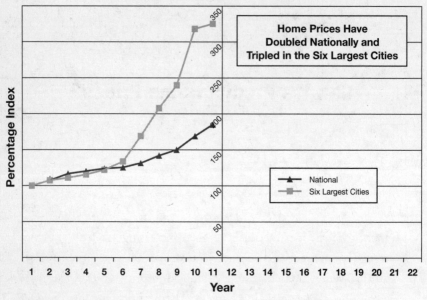

Source of Data: *Statistical Yearbook (2005)*

foreseeable future. If this were the plot of some physical attribute like population or the number of crimes in a society, that might be the most reasonable approach. If we applied such a method to this graph we could forecast that prices might travel a trajectory like that shown in Figure 1.2.

If this is indeed the correct forecast of expected prices, then one can conclude that the current housing market is not overvalued and, in fact, current prices represent quite a bargain relative to where prices might be headed in the future. If we were certain of this forecast, it would be easy to make money by simply buying as much real estate as possible with as much debt as possible and then sitting back and waiting for the market prices to increase. While this is not the most sophisticated forecasting method in the world, it does seem that this

Figure 1.2: Historical Trend-Line Forecast

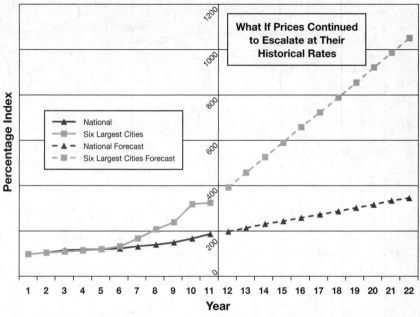

Source of Data: *Statistical Yearbook (2005)*

is exactly what many buyers are actually doing. At current price levels the investment math just doesn't work on many real estate projects unless we assume substantial price appreciation in the future.

If housing were guaranteed to double or triple again over the next eleven years as it has in the past, then an investor could put 10 percent down and gain a return of between ten to thirty times his money in a little more than a decade. Certainly, properly priced markets do not allow such unusual profit opportunities without real effort and risk-taking.

Maybe it is not smart to look at real estate prices in isolation. Let me continue the analysis by showing you what interest rates did over this period (see Figure 1.3).

Figure 1.3: Historical Interest Rates

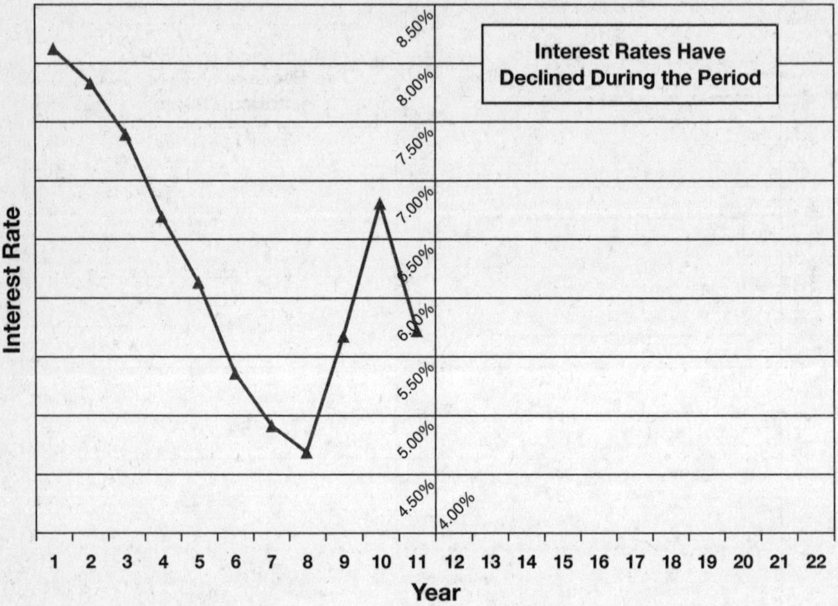

Source of Data: *Statistical Yearbook (2005)*

If we knew or had a feeling for what interest rates might do in the future, we might have a much different forecast of housing prices. But we run into the same problem. Interest rates are almost impossible to predict. There are tens of thousands of traders on Wall Street trying to do just that and very few consistently have any success with their forecasts.

What other factors might influence housing prices?

In Figure 1.4 we see the population is aging throughout the time period, and it would not be unreasonable to assume that this demographic trend will continue into the future. Does this provide us some valuable insight as to the direction of house prices?

What we have graphed in Figure 1.1 are not just physical items

Figure 1.4: Aging of the Population

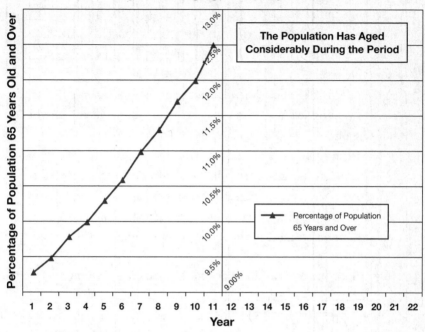

Source of Data: *Statistical Yearbook (2005)*

like the number of cattle in the country or the incidence of an illness, but rather real market prices. Predicting prices is not as simple as trend-line analysis that just draws a line through previous history. The reason is that in pure markets, if your best estimation of the future was significantly higher prices, you would be able to achieve fairly riskless and effortless profits by simply buying today and selling tomorrow, a strategy many housing investors are trying to implement today. But real markets are not that generous. When markets price assets correctly, they eliminate any method of effortlessly generating a profit at little to no risk. That is the beauty of a perfect market—no one can profit without hard work and risk taking. The value we create in the housing market is not in trading assets but in building or renovating them. In other words, there is little to no real productivity in buying and selling the same asset quickly and so there should be no real unusually positive return from doing so.

This "efficient" theory of markets, that prevents simple and effortless trading profits, leads to a completely different forecast of housing prices.

We see in Figure 1.5 a more rational forecast of expected home prices if we believe the housing market behaves rationally. But it is clear that the economist's efficient market hypothesis creates a much different forecast of future prices than that of someone who simply constructs a trend-line analysis and assumes that historical growth will continue

Figures1.5: Flat-Line Forecast of Housing Prices

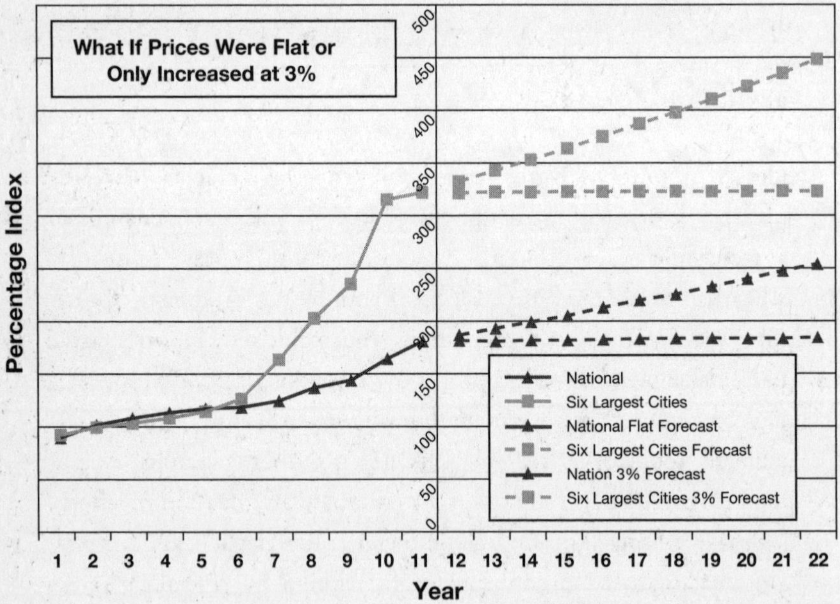

Source of Data: *Statistical Yearbook (2005)*

into the future. Instead of doubling and tripling home values over time, now it is very hard to beat inflation from any future returns.

And what of the additional information we discovered on the level and general direction of interest rates and the aging of the population? This is where markets become all-powerful. While this information definitely can have an effect on the pricing of homes, market theory tells us it is already incorporated into the price you are paying today for a home. It's not as if you are the only person on the planet who knows that the population is aging. If there is a vacation-home effect or a downsizing effect from this aging pattern that affects house prices, you can assume it has already been reflected in the price. In other words, the price is assumed to take into account that the population is aging and its affect on future housing demand and supply.

Now what if I told you I could do a more accurate job of predicting where the next eleven years of housing prices in this graph will actually go? What if I told you that I could predict almost exactly what the actual average house price will be in the out years of this graph? Here (Figure 1.6) is my prediction of what the prices in the out years will be for both the nation as a whole and for the six largest cities.

When I show Figure 1.6 at conferences I often give members of the audience an opportunity to bet with me as to whether I will turn out to be right in my rather negative forecast. In essence, I am predicting that all prices will return to just about the level they were at prior to the boom in prices. Because of the perceived difficulty in making accurate predictions as well as the generally pessimistic forecast I have presented, I usually get a number of parties interested in wagering that I have overstated my predictive abilities.

But they end up losing their bet against me. My prediction is 100 percent accurate. The prices that result are exactly as I have

Figure 1.6: Prediction of Home Prices, Nationally and in the Six Largest Cities

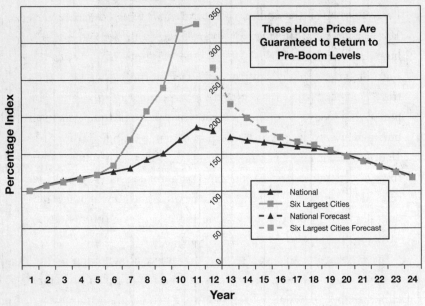

These Home Prices Are Guaranteed to Return to Pre-Boom Levels

National
Six Largest Cities
National Forecast
Six Largest Cities Forecast

Percentage Index

Year

Source of Data: *Statistical Yearbook (2005)*

predicted them. And there is no margin of error. Each of the predicted prices is exactly right. Not only did I predict the peak and the ensuing crash in real estate prices, I did it with no errors.

How is this possible? Remember how Paul Newman was able to pick horse-race winners in the movie *The Sting*? That's right, he made his predictions after the races were over. He didn't predict the future, which is always a tricky business, but rather made a much better go of it by predicting the past.

I apologize because I have not been completely honest with you up to now. I, too, have not been predicting the future, but rather have done an exemplary job of predicting past prices that have already occurred with certainty. This chart is not the level of home prices in the

United States, but rather the level of home prices in Japan. And as you can see in Figure 1.7, which has the correct years labeled on the x-axis, I was not predicting the future, but Japan's past. My "predictions" are 100 percent accurate. Japan already had this exact experience in their housing boom and bust over the last two decades.

After experiencing a doubling of home prices nationwide and a tripling of home prices in their largest cities, prices collapsed to their pre-boom levels. This was a real market bubble growing and then bursting, and the decline was much more than a simple correction of 10 or 15 percent. Japan's biggest cities saw a decline of 65 percent from their peak values while the entire nation saw average declines of 40 percent. Individual homes in Tokyo saw declines of 80 percent and more.

Figure 1.7: Home Prices in Japan

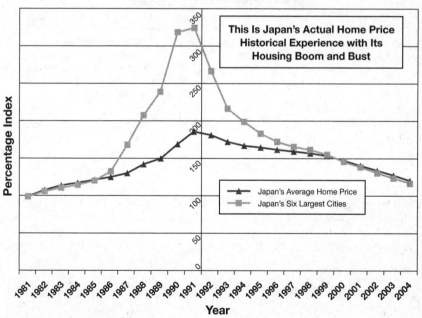

This Is Japan's Actual Home Price Historical Experience with Its Housing Boom and Bust

Japan's Average Home Price
Japan's Six Largest Cities

Source: *Japan Statistical Yearbook (2005)*

This example could stop here and it would be useful because it has demonstrated two important points: (1) housing bubbles are not theoretical exercises but have actually occurred in the very recent past and have caused trillions of dollars in damage, and (2) when forecasting prices, don't just look at flat and increasing prices but rather assign some probability to real declines in price and be sure you have planned adequately for such circumstances.

Let us look at Figure 1.8 to see what the U.S. numbers look like for the current period.

As you can see, the United States experience over the last eleven years is not that different from what Japan experienced before their crash. Here in the United States, housing prices have

Figure 1.8: U.S. Housing Prices for the Nation and the Six Largest Cities

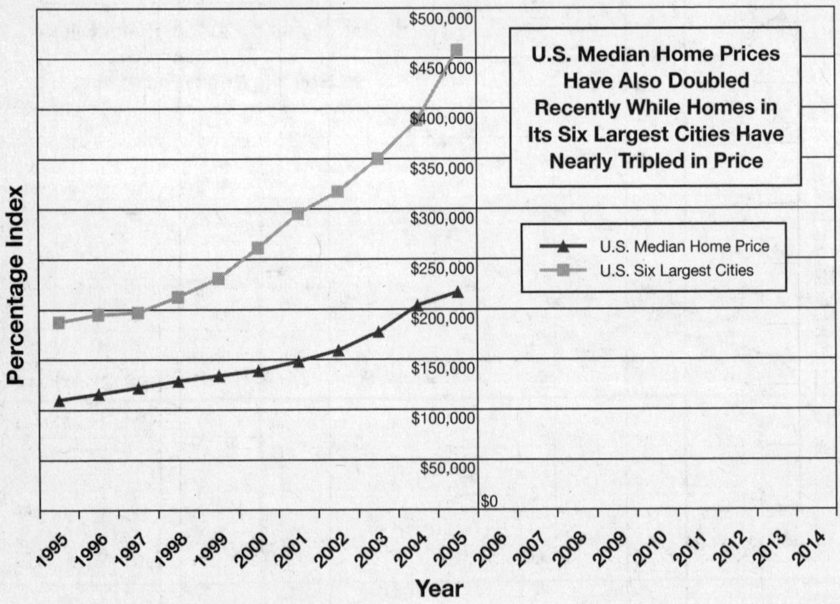

> **U.S. Median Home Prices Have Also Doubled Recently While Homes in Its Six Largest Cities Have Nearly Tripled in Price**

Legend:
- U.S. Median Home Price
- U.S. Six Largest Cities

Y-axis: Percentage Index ($0 to $500,000)
X-axis: Year (1995 to 2014)

Source of Data: *UCLA Anderson Macroeconomic Forecast*

doubled nationally in eleven years, and homes in our largest cities have nearly tripled in price. This is almost identical to the experience in Japan before their crash. Of course, there is no reason why the United States has to follow exactly Japan's pattern. But let us continue the analysis and see if there are any other similarities between these two countries in these respective time periods.

As Figure 1.9 shows, in the United States, as in Japan before their crash, interest rates have been falling.

Interest rates are a very big part of the housing price story and we will return to discuss them in more detail in chapter 7. But the Japanese experience highlights that interest rates, just like housing

Figure 1.9: Interest Rates

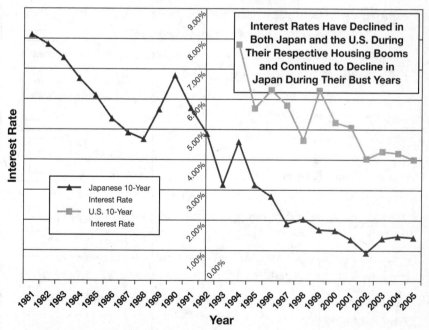

Interest Rates Have Declined in Both Japan and the U.S. During Their Respective Housing Booms and Continued to Decline in Japan During Their Bust Years

Japanese 10-Year Interest Rate

U.S. 10-Year Interest Rate

Interest Rate

Year

Source: *Japan Statistical Yearbook (2005)*

prices, are a market and therefore very difficult to forecast. I doubt anyone in Japan back in 1991 would have expected interest rates on ten-year government bonds to continue to decline till they reached 1 percent in 2002. The U.S. market in which bonds trade, where investors try to profit from variability of interest rates, is huge, with transactions amounting to many trillions of dollars every year. Therefore, the same rules apply. One cannot assume that rates will go up in the future or that they will decline. They can do either. Thus, the best guess of where they will be in the future is exactly where they are now. If that were not true, someone would buy or sell bonds in the market and earn an effortless profit, and that is something we realize that proper market pricing prevents.

As can be seen in the chart, interest rates during the U.S. real estate boom have declined very similarly to the rate decline in Japan during their boom years. Interest rates in the United States in the future could increase, decrease, or stay the same. An increase in interest rates could threaten the housing market because of the large number of adjustable-rate mortgages (ARMs) currently being issued. If rates increase, ARM borrowers are going to face significantly higher monthly mortgage payments in the future, as soon as their mortgages reset.

But what happens if rates go down from here? Most homeowners would probably think that this would be good for the housing market because they are used to interest rates declining and homeowners saving on monthly mortgage costs through refinancing at the lower rate. The assumption might be that if rates go down, not only can the homeowner refinance at lower rates, but more first-time buyers will qualify to buy homes at even higher prices, thus leading to further housing price increases and the opportunity for even greater borrowing and consumption.

But this is not exactly what will happen if rates continue to decline from today's current levels. If ten-year Treasuries continue to decline below 4.5 percent, even as the Federal Reserve has raised the very short-term Fed funds rate, it may signal something much more serious. Typically, when the Fed raises short-term rates, long-term rates like the ten-year Treasury increase also. Here they seem to be moving in opposite directions.

We have all heard explanations of why this very large and very sophisticated Treasury bond market might not be moving properly. Most often, blame is placed on the Chinese for either selling us too many inexpensive goods or buying too many of our Treasury bonds. These are feasible explanations, but if they are true, one has to believe that the Treasury bond market is not tied to fundamentals, or that an unexpected inflow of money from a foreign power can move its yield to places not congruent with people's actual expectations of the future. For example, people might want to believe that inflation will be under control and average 3 percent over the next ten years and that the economy is in good shape and will grow at 3.5 percent over the same period. The problem of course is that if this is true, then an investor in ten-year Treasuries would expect to earn something closer to 6.5 percent per year, not the 4.5 percent that Treasuries are currently yielding.

If the 4.5 percent current Treasury yield is correct, it is telling us something much darker about our country's future. If fundamentals are driving its yield, then it must be that people either have a much lower expectation of inflation going forward or don't believe the economy is going to grow at anywhere near a 3.5 percent rate. Both of these possibilities could spell real trouble for the housing market in the United States.

If general inflation is less than 3 percent per year in the future, it is going to be very hard for home prices to grow at rates higher than that. If the long Treasury bond rate is at 4.5 percent and is right, it means that the market is not only expecting very low inflation, but that there is a real probability of deflation, a period when prices of goods decrease each year. Again, if handled properly by our monetary authorities, deflation for an economy may not be as bad as it sounds. But again, homeowners should be extremely wary of general deflation in the economy because it is hard to imagine homes continuing their upward spiral in price if all other goods are declining in value. In addition, housing debt can become quite burdensome during deflationary periods.

There is one other explanation of today's unusually low Treasuries rate environment. If the Treasury market is not expecting significantly less inflation, maybe it is signaling that it expects much less real growth in the economy. If inflation is assumed to hold at 3 percent per year, and Treasuries trade near 4 percent yields, it says that real yields will only be 1 percent per year. This is not much of a real return if a country were going to be experiencing real GDP growth of 3 to 4 percent per year. Maybe the Treasury yield is telling us that we may be facing a much leaner future. Maybe investors in the Treasuries market are expecting GDP growth over the next ten years of 1 to 2 percent, or maybe they are expecting a recession with negative real growth to the economy.

This seems awfully unreasonable given the good growth record of the recent past in our country. But who can say how much of that recent growth has been due to the dramatic housing price run-up? Experts estimate GDP growth would be from 1 to 2 percent lower if home prices stopped rising in the future, and I believe zero or negative real economic growth would result. The real estate industry would slow, as would the mortgage and banking industries. Home Depot may not have to open at eight o'clock on Sunday mornings. And boat and car sales would slow as homeowners would be unable to borrow money against their homes and spend it on themselves.

Renovation work and teardowns and condo building would stop. And consumers would feel a whole lot poorer if their homes dropped dramatically in value, and they would then consume less.

There is another similarity between Japan and the United States, as shown in Figure 1.10.

The United States already has 12 percent of its population over the age of 65, which is similar to the percentage when Japan's real estate decline began, and our aging problem is forecasted to grow much worse over the next forty years, with 21 percent of the U.S. population being 65 years or older by 2050.

Figure 1.10: Aging of Population—Percentage of Population 65 Years of Age and Over

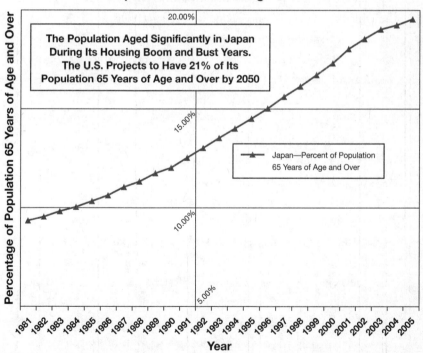

The Population Aged Significantly in Japan During Its Housing Boom and Bust Years. The U.S. Projects to Have 21% of Its Population 65 Years of Age and Over by 2050

Japan—Percent of Population 65 Years of Age and Over

Source of Data: *Japan Statistical Yearbook (2005)*

The world is divided today between countries whose populations are aging, on average, and those that are much younger. Much of the developing world, including India and many of the Muslim countries, are enjoying a baby boom of their own, but the average age of this boom is currently only 15 to 25 years. China is an exception in the developing world, as it severely restricted birth rates decades ago and now has a much older average population than most countries in the developing world. And the eldest in much of the developing world are only forty-five years old because of sickness, inadequate health care, and early death. Therefore the average age in the developing world is much younger than in the advanced world.

All of the industrialized countries of the world have much more advanced average ages. Better health care leading to longer life spans and the aging of the original post-World War II baby boom are the reasons. But among the industrialized nations, Japan is unique. The Japanese aged the fastest and the soonest. They lost many of their citizens in World War II, enjoyed less of a baby boom after the war, and now have a significant percentage of their population over 65 years of age. So Japan is interesting to look at because its people are not only aging like us, but are ahead of us on the curve. They are experiencing an aging of their population that is about ten to fifteen years ahead of where we will eventually be. Again, it does not mean that we will react similarly, but it would be a mistake not to at least try to understand the effects.

As populations age, a greater percentage enter retirement age. And as these previously actively working participants in the economy shift to retirement, their economic production drops dramatically, and they begin to consume rather than save. In effect, the savings rates among this retiree group can go negative, as they could very well consume more than they produce. This is the whole foundation for saving toward your retirement—at some point you are expected to stop working and live off your savings.

This can be very bad news for the overall economy. Because of the baby boom, more people may be leaving the productive workforce than entering it. Or at least, those leaving may be temporarily more senior and better trained than the next generation that is rapidly trying to replace their productive capacity. To the extent that baby boomers continue to work part-time in retirement or to pursue entrepreneurial second careers, this effect is less pronounced. If baby boomers begin to retire early and cash out of generous private and public pension plans, the effect on the economy could be much worse. Evidence on the front wave of baby boomers in the United States who are reaching 57 and 58 years of age suggests that many are indeed retiring early, but that many are also continuing to pursue work in some more entrepreneurial ventures, including renovating houses and selling them.

If we lose our extremely productive and hardworking baby boomers from the workforce this may have a devastating impact on GDP growth. America has a large immigrant population that is younger and anxious to get to work, but a large percentage of it is poorly educated and their alien work status is hurting their efforts at finding productive work. And if GDP growth slows as our population ages, this cannot be good for home prices. Home prices in the long run reflect the long-run productivity of a country because rents are typically closely related to incomes, and land values themselves are a measure of the productive ability of property in the society. Land goes up in value in a country because somebody has developed a more productive use for it in creating earnings and cash flows.

As we have seen, Japan went into a prolonged period of declining home prices, deflation, and lower interest rates as their population aged. Their economy has suffered for almost fifteen years since its peak. There are many explanations of why it has taken Japan so long to recover. Clearly, Japan's banks were very slow to report the significant amount of bad loans they had generated during their bubble period of housing and stock market booms. The Japanese banks grew tremendously during the boom period, added a huge volume of loans to their books, but unfortunately many of these were bad loans.

Japan is different from the United States in that their government controls much of their economy. It is a much more hierarchical, top-down society and economy than the United States. When its banks got in trouble with bad loans, it is not that its government's regulators didn't know. Rather, it was the government that was calling the shots at the banks. Under the Japanese system, individual corporations took orders from the banks, who received instructions from the Ministry of Finance, which was the main government body regulating the economy through the banks. The Ministry of Finance was slow to force Japanese banks to disclose their bad loans because it would have bankrupted a number of them. Rather, they played a slow waiting game in which earnings from other bank activities over time quietly replaced the losses from the bad loans and preserved the equity of the Japanese banks. But such a slow bleed of losses from their bad loans prevented the Japanese banks from being overly aggressive in their other lending and virtually assured that Japan's economy would languish in the doldrums of a lengthy recession.

Some might argue that the United States is nothing like Japan and that our government would never allow banks to sit on bad loans while the economy and home prices collapsed. But the United States is becoming more and more like Japan every day. It was only twenty-five years ago that Japan dominated the United States in automobile manufacture and Americans were wondering if there was anything we could do to better adopt what we thought at the time was a superior Japanese management style. And the changes did not stop on the shop floor or in the executive office. American industry argued that Japan had developed a superior political system in which industry and government were more like partners than adversaries, the typical description of their relationship in the United States.

It appeared to many here that if we could get government off the back of industry we could accomplish a great deal more. Government regulation was viewed as unproductive, and our biggest corporations were cleared to get much bigger in order to compete in the global economy, especially with Japan.

And that is what we did. But what have we given up? We now have a government that is much more a partner of industry, but has it gone too far? Wall Street collapsed in early 2000, partly because of a lack of proper governmental supervision of our investment banks, their research staffs, and the entire initial public offering process. Enron led an entire wave of corporate bankruptcies that resulted when government entrusted corporate supervision to the corrupted accounting industry. The stock market, unsupervised, created a dot.com bubble of mythic proportions, only to cause trillions of dollars of losses when it finally imploded. Many Americans still have not regained their confidence in the integrity of the American financial system, part of the reason for the recent huge flow of funds into residential real estate. And in the latest example of poor oversight of corporate power, the SEC commissioner who straightened up the mess after the stock market bubble burst has been replaced with a supporter of the very same corporate crowd that is trying to avoid any substantial regulation of their activities.

If America is becoming more like Japan and our banks and corporations are getting cozier with and closer to our government, this may be very bad for our economic outlook going forward, especially in regard to how we react to a possible bursting of the real estate bubble in this country. Maybe American regulators like the Office of Federal Housing Enterprise Oversight (OFHEO) and the Federal Deposit Insurance Corporation (FDIC) and the Federal Reserve are not sufficiently independent from politics and corporate power to properly regulate the banks, Fannie Mae, and Freddie Mac. Maybe by lowering regulation we are increasing the odds of our ending up like Japan. Not only is the probability of experiencing an unsustainable economic bubble increased, but the odds of someone quickly and decisively stepping in to correct the situation as it deflates is much less. For the first time it is conceivable that our banks are being allowed to continue to add suspect mortgage loans to their balance sheets with the proviso that if they get in trouble the regulators will be very slow to step in and correct the situation. Unfortunately, if this is the case, the American economy will suffer tremendously in a housing downturn as trillions of bad real estate loans hang over the entire banking sector.

It is not clear that America today would react that differently to a bubble-bursting crisis than the Japanese did. Even if you optimistically (and naïvely) believe our government is independent of political pressure brought on it by industry and the banks, the Fed may be very slow to force banks to recognize losses and thus push the problem out for years. In an attempt to protect some of our biggest banks and possibly avert a bank run on the entire system, the Fed may choose to punish the American economy for years as it struggles slowly out of the loan morass it created during this real estate bubble. No, the story Japan has to tell is not a pretty one, but unless we are expected to repeat their troubled history we had best do something differently with our future. The time to deal with a real estate bubble is not when it starts deflating but rather when it is growing uncontrollably. Some intervention of common sense and analysis now will prevent a great deal of heartache and human suffering later.

2

Evidence of a Bubble?

There is much discussion today about whether the housing market in the United States is trapped in a bubble of unrealistic and unsustainable prices or whether the current high prices are correct and reflect sound underlying market fundamentals. Unfortunately, few people have taken the time to thoroughly examine the evidence available to see whether it supports their position, and most of this debate has occurred in magazines, newspapers, and on television talk shows that do not provide a proper format to allow an in-depth discussion of the issue. Television sound bites about housing bubbles and housing crashes attract viewers, but television is a poor medium to address the complex nature of how housing prices are actually determined. Different theories, both in support of the bubble premise and against it, are discussed, but no attempt is made to see if individual theories actually help explain the housing price data we have witnessed to date or if they can stand up to tough critical questioning from experts in the field.

It is no coincidence that many of the biggest housing price bulls today who express the strongest positive opinions regarding the health of the housing market happen to work for real estate, housing construction, or mortgage industry organizations such as the National Association of Realtors (NAR).

The chief economist of the NAR recently published a book entitled *Are You Missing the Real Estate Boom? Why Home Values and Other Real Estate Investments Will Climb Through the End of the Decade*. Regardless of whether the author honestly believes this thesis or not, it seems inappropriate for someone with such an obvious conflict of interest to opine publicly as to the reasonableness of home prices. Turning to the NAR's chief economist for advice on housing prices is like asking the devil whether he likes warm climates. You would do much better to seek the opinions of people not so directly involved in the issue you are trying to explore.

Formal academic researchers are much better able to take the time to apply the needed academic rigor to explore a complicated question such as the proper level of housing prices. Academics should also have one other great advantage in examining this question: they should be unbiased. For whatever reason, there has been very little academic research conducted in the field of residential real estate. Throughout this book I will present the findings of the academic community in this area. But I will extend the current debate by critiquing some of the academics' findings and suggesting theories of my own that better explain the historical data.

In writing this book I have taken the time necessary to describe in detail the various theories of whether there is a housing bubble or not. This simply cannot be accomplished in a two-minute appearance on television or conveyed in three paragraphs of a magazine article. The good news is it is a really fascinating story to tell. The reader who is already familiar with the arguments presented will appreciate seeing which theories actually can withstand tough scrutiny and which do a poor job of explaining the recent high home prices.

There are literally millions of pieces of data that can be analyzed in trying to determine the reasonableness of home prices today. It can be overwhelming to examine the countless presentations and reports that purport to explain the current housing market. Therefore, summarized here are the most important and most illuminating presentations of the historical data on housing prices that need explaining. This data encompasses more than a century of price data and includes price information from not only most of the major metropolitan areas in the United States, but also housing information from many of the countries of the world. If I can find a theory of home prices that explains this historical evidence perhaps I can help explain today's high prices and make some judgment as to the reasonableness and sustainability of today's home prices.

Here then is the evidence. I will discuss throughout the book what possible explanations there are for this evidence and whether it supports the bubble theory or contradicts it. But I will let the evidence guide me rather than follow preconceived notions as to whether housing is overpriced or not.

The easiest housing information to gather and report is the actual median price paid for existing single family houses that were sold each year in the past. This data is presented in Figure 2.1.

While this chart is indeed illuminating, one can draw two quite different conclusions if it is viewed in isolation. The bullish housing investor can argue from this evidence that housing prices have always gone up in price in the past and therefore there is no reason to conclude that they will not continue to do so in the future. A bullish real estate investor could easily conclude from looking at this graph that it is wise to buy real estate with maximum leverage regardless of the price paid since it always increases in the future. He might

Figure 2.1: U.S. Median Existing Home Nominal Sales Price

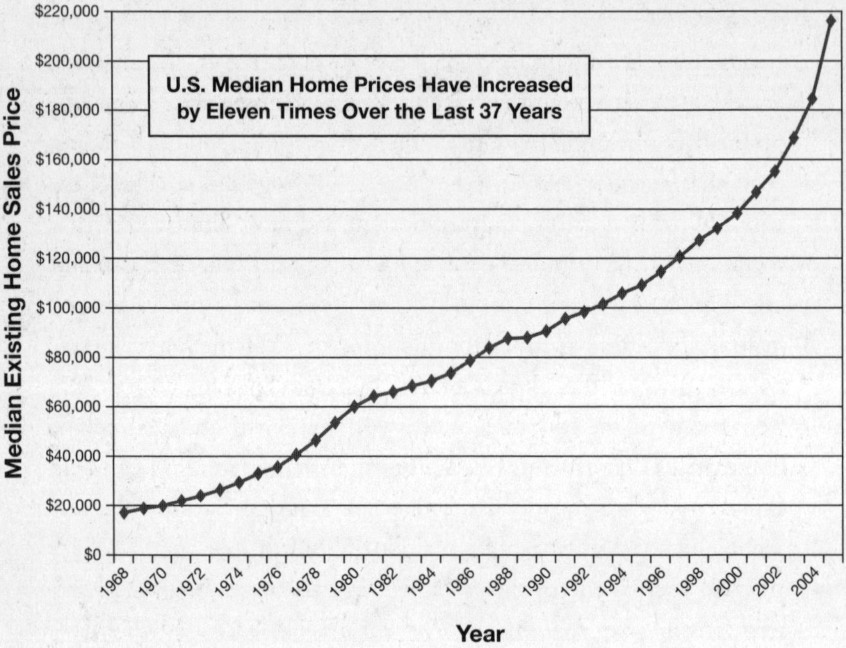

U.S. Median Home Prices Have Increased
by Eleven Times Over the Last 37 Years

Source of Data: *National Association of Realtors, Existing Home Sales Survey*

decide to pay such a high price for investment properties that he loses money each month with the hope of recouping his losses in the future once prices rise. Investors will accept negative monthly cash flows on properties if they expect future price appreciation to bail them out.

The housing bear draws quite different conclusions when he looks at the chart. He is amazed that prices seem to have increased every year for thirty-seven years in a row. His knowledge of other markets makes him extremely suspicious of any market that only goes one direction—up! He knows that trees don't grow to the sky. He also knows that housing prices have to have some correlation to other real economic fundamentals such as family incomes, potential rental incomes, and the economy, and he knows these fundamental factors have not been growing anywhere near as fast as these historical home prices. Lastly, he wonders how a commodity like a house could appreciate so rapidly when he knows that the cost of building homes has not appreciated anywhere near as much.

If our analysis stopped here, clearly we would not have contributed much to the debate on home prices. But it is illuminating to see that a simple chart of historical home prices can support both sides of the argument, a necessary condition for a full-fledged fight over who is right—the bulls or the bears.

The historical prices we have presented need further analysis to uncover their true amount of appreciation. The most important element causing a distortion to these reported results is general price inflation in the economy. As monetarists like Milton Friedman first realized, general inflation occurs when the government prints money to fund government deficits. Too much currency chasing the same amount of goods and services leads to the price of everything on average appreciating in price. But these price increases are not real. You can't consume more goods in the future by selling something at the higher price because any good you wish to consume has also inflated in price by the same amount. Dollars have devalued, but all goods and services have the same "real" price over time.

So to better see what "real" home prices have been historically, over time, we need to adjust the prices for general inflation. We need to deduct that portion of the house price appreciation each year that is solely due to just general price inflation and the government's printing of currency.

As can be seen in Figure 2.2, housing appreciation back in the eighties was almost fully explained by general price inflation, but recently, home prices have been increasing much faster than general price inflation.

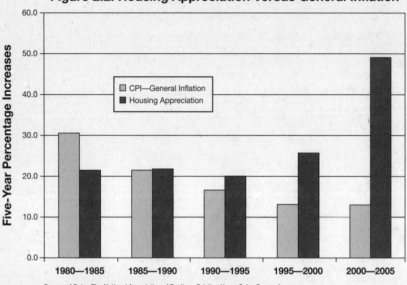

Figure 2.2: Housing Appreciation Versus General Inflation

Source of Data: *The National Association of Realtors, Existing Home Sales Survey for Home Prices,* and *Bureau of Labor Statistics*

In my first book, *The Coming Crash in the Housing Market,* I performed an analysis of what real home prices looked like after adjusting for inflation for the last forty years. Now there is even better data on the topic. Robert J. Shiller of Yale University in the second edition of his book *Irrational Exuberance* has gone back over one hundred years and has adjusted reported home sales prices for general inflation in the economy. In addition he has kept the quality of homes constant by examining the prices that a single property sold for over time in numerous sale transactions. Figure 2.3 shows what real home prices have done over the last century after controlling for general inflation and maintaining constant quality constraints.

Figure 2.3 tells quite a different story from Figure 2.1 that doesn't control for inflation and home quality. Shiller's data make it much more difficult for the housing bull to suggest that things look

Figure 2.3: Long-Term Real Housing Price Index After Adjusting for Inflation

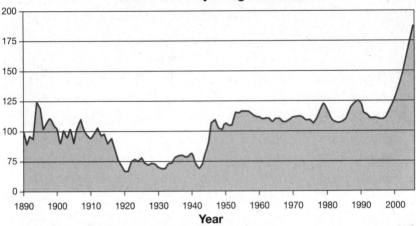

Year

Source: Shiller, Robert J., *Irrational Exuberance, Second Edition.* Princeton University Press. Reprinted by permission of Princeton University Press.

completely normal today. Examining real housing prices over time highlights that our experience over the last nine years is dramatically different from what has preceded.

There are really two rather shocking conclusions that can be drawn from this chart. One, housing prices recently have appreciated significantly in real terms after adjusting for inflation, and two, housing prices have been relatively stable for the hundred years prior to 1996. The second finding, that real home prices have been so stable, surprises us, because we mistakenly believed that they were not only volatile, but ever-increasing.

The flatness of the real historical price data presented here tells another important story. Whenever a boom in real estate has occurred in the past, it was eventually followed by a bust: real prices always returned to normal levels. It is not fair to say that the current boom will fully reverse itself, but it is accurate to say that if it does not, it will be the first time in a century that a boom in real prices actually stuck.

In addition to the flatness of the real price data, the chart shows how large the recent price move has been relative to history. A 50 percent real price increase may not sound big to people familiar with 15 percent inflation, but, remember, these are "real" increases already adjusted for inflation. Real productivity increases 1 to 2 percent a year, real wages are lucky to grow at 0.5 percent per year, real population growth is close to 1 percent a year, and here we are talking about a 50 percent increase in real home prices since 1997. This is quite a different order of magnitude. You can judge the magnitude of this increase by contrasting it with the historical volatility of the real housing data prior to 1996. As seen in the chart it was unusual in the past for historical real housing prices to exhibit more than a 20 percent increase, and as we said, these increases always turned out to be temporary.

Shiller's work is important because it shifts the debate from having to explain why housing prices have always appreciated historically to why, in real terms, they never appreciated until the last nine years. This presentation of the real price data seems to be very strong evidence of a housing bubble. For housing bulls to claim that there is not a bubble they must produce reasonable explanations of why home prices that were relatively flat for a hundred years have suddenly shot up. I will explore some of their possible theories in chapter 5.

But this chart also asks another important question. What is it about 1997 that caused such a dramatic shift in how home prices appreciated? Such a bold move in historical price data is helpful in our finding an explanation for the historical price change because it so clearly points us to the departure point, in this case 1997. We need only explore what changed in 1997 and we can begin to form our own new theory of what actually drives home prices.

But what if 1997 was not the real inflection point? What if real home prices started accelerating in value much earlier? To see this we must make one further adjustment to Shiller's historical data.

It turns out that when you purchase a home in the United States you are actually buying two different assets, both of great economic value. You have acquired the house itself and the land it sits on, but you also have acquired a very valuable tax shield. Because the Internal Revenue Service allows you to deduct mortgage interest from your taxable income, when you buy a home you also buy this tax shield. And this tax shield has dropped dramatically in value since 1981, when interest rates and inflation peaked. In 1981, this tax shield represented as much as 30 percent of the value you might pay for a primary residence, but today this same tax shield in a world of much lower inflation is only worth approximately 9 percent of the purchase price.

This means that even though total prices paid appeared to be flat from 1981 to 1997 in Shiller's data, the portion of the purchase price paid for the home itself, ignoring the tax shield, was actually rising quite rapidly. As nominal interest rates and inflation declined after 1981, the value associated with the tax shield declined and masked what was an underlying appreciation in the housing asset itself.

This can be seen in Figure 2.4, which is a plot of real home prices after subtracting the value of the tax shield.

As Figure 2.4 indicates, it is 1981, not 1997, that marks the beginning of the current housing boom. This is a very important improvement to Shiller's analysis. It still confirms that housing prices have been relatively stable for most of the last hundred years because, prior to the 1970s, inflation and the value of the tax shield were quite low. It also confirms his findings that we are experiencing an unusual, once in a century, real boom in prices.

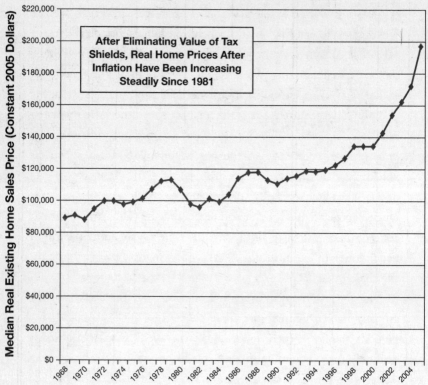

Figure 2.4: Real Home Prices

After Eliminating Value of Tax Shields, Real Home Prices After Inflation Have Been Increasing Steadily Since 1981

Source of Data: *National Association of Realtors, Existing Home Sales Survey for Home Prices,* and *Bureau of Labor Statistics*

This may turn out to be very important to our understanding of the cause of the current boom. Now, we can focus our attention on the year 1981 to see if we can think of something that changed that year that may have had a real impact on home prices after allowing for the value of the inherent tax shield of home ownership.

The year 1981 was interesting for many reasons, but to an economist it was a watershed year for one very important reason. This was the year that inflation and nominal interest rates peaked. Interest rates hit an all-time high when the thirty-year mortgage rate hit 16.6 percent. Mortgage rates have been in almost constant decline since then. This new analysis of the historical data seems to point to the very real possibility that the interest rate decline is somehow responsible for the current housing price boom.

Before the housing bulls suggest that, of course, lower interest rates cause higher home prices, let us remind them that most of the interest rate decline we have experienced since 1981 was nominal, not real. If interest rates went from 15 percent to 5 percent over the period, and inflation eased by the same 10 percent, then real interest rates didn't change at all. If real interest rates didn't change, then real home prices, after deducting the value of the tax shield, should not have increased one dollar in real value since 1981, all other things being equal. This is such a dramatic statement that I will return to it in chapter 7 and explore the issue more fully. And I will ask the question, if real interest rates didn't change when nominal rates declined in 1981, what did change that could have led to higher home prices?

And so, all I have done is take readily available data on home prices over time and apply simple economic analysis to try to uncover what "true" or real home values have been doing recently. I conclude that home prices are up substantially in real terms after being fairly flat for most of the century. And the current real price boom in home values, ignoring the value of the tax shield that ownership provides, started its acceleration in 1981, the year nominal interest rates began their descent. Let us examine other pricing evidence from a number of metropolitan areas, as well as evidence from overseas, to see if we might uncover further clues as to what might be driving prices higher in the current boom.

3

More Evidence from the
Cities of the World

Some of the most striking evidence of a possible explanation for the current housing boom comes from a city-by-city comparison of home prices in the recent past. As I suggested in my first book, home prices should have some relation to the rental income the property might earn annually, regardless of whether the homeowner intends to lease the property or live in it himself.

If the homeowner rents the home out, the cash flow obtained, after allowing for expenditures like maintenance costs and property taxes, can be used in a traditional economic analysis to determine whether the cash return justifies the price being paid. If the buyer chooses to live in the home, then the expected, but foregone, rental income can be thought of as a cost of occupying the home and can be included in a similar economic analysis to determine the true value of the house.

Therefore, a shorthand way to assess the reasonableness of a home's price as compared to its potential rental cash flow is to talk about a housing price-earnings ratio. The housing P/E is the home price or market value divided by its potential annual rental income.

If you pay $240,000 for a home that you can rent out for $2,000 a month, or $24,000 a year, then the home is said to have a housing P/E of 10. If the home appreciates in value to $264,000, but the potential rental income stream remains unchanged, then the home's P/E has increased from 10 to 11.

Table 3.1 shows the average housing P/E multiple for many of those cities that have seen a larger than national average expansion in their housing P/Es. Something dramatic has happened over the five-year period. The average housing multiple for the entire nation has increased nearly 47 percent during this period, from 11.6 to approximately 17.1.

This is a huge increase in a market-determined measure of pricing reasonableness for two reasons. First, it is a real increase, because inflation does not enter into the calculation of housing P/Es. Inflation impacts both the numerator, the housing price, and the denominator, the first year's rental income stream, equally. Similarly, a nominal decline in interest rates should have no impact on this valuation measure as long as real underlying rates remain unchanged. To effect a change in the market's average housing multiple, one of four things has to occur: real rates of interest have to change; real expected growth rates in the rental income stream have to expand or contract; people have to experience a substantial increase in their fundamental desire to pay for housing; or the housing supply has to be dramatically, and unexpectedly, constrained during the period.

It is true that over the last five years, the average multiple paid for homes has expanded by some 47 percent. But this is not the most amazing element present in this data. In the year 2000, when the average city had a home P/E multiple of 11.7, most of the cities in America had housing P/E multiples in a very tight range around that average—from 10.6 to 12.8. By 2005, although the national average

Table 3.1 Average Housing P/E Multiples (Home Price/Rental Income) for Many of the Major Metropolitan Areas of the U.S. with Housing P/E Multiples That Have Expanded Faster Than the National Average.

Metropolitan Area	Home Price/ Rental Income 2000	Home Price/ Rental Income 2005	Multiple Expansion
San Francisco, CA	12.5	34.1	172.8%
West Palm Beach—Boca Raton, FL	11.6	29.4	153.4%
San Jose, CA	14.1	34.0	141.1%
New York—Northern New Jersey, NY—NJ	10.6	25.4	139.6%
Sacramento—Yolo, CA	11.5	26.5	130.4%
Orange County, CA	11.8	25.7	117.8%
San Diego, CA	13.5	28.9	114.1%
Miami, FL	11.5	24.5	113.0%
Fort Lauderdale, FL	11.6	24.5	111.2%
Boston, MA—NH PMSA	11.5	23.9	107.8%
Orlando, FL	11.9	24.3	104.2%
Nassau—Suffolk, NY	10.8	21.9	102.8%
Los Angeles—Long Beach, CA	12.3	24.9	102.4%
Las Vegas, NV	11.8	23.4	98.3%
Riverside—San Bernardino, CA	11.9	23.1	94.1%
Oakland, CA	11.4	21.7	90.4%
Washington, D.C.	11.2	19.6	75.0%
Newark, NJ	10.9	18.4	68.8%
Tampa—St. Petersburg—Clearwater, FL	11.4	19.0	66.7%
Middlesex—Somerset, NJ	11.6	19.1	64.7%
Phoenix—Mesa, AZ	12.2	19.7	61.5%
Minneapolis—St. Paul, MN	12.0	18.7	55.8%
Baltimore, MD	11.5	17.7	53.9%
Hartford, CT	11.2	17.2	53.6%
Chicago, IL	11.4	17.4	52.6%
Seattle—Bellevue—Everett, WA	12.8	19.0	48.4%
United States Average	**11.6**	**17.1**	**47.4%**

Source of Data: UCLA Anderson Macroeconomic Forecast

Source of Analysis: Author

had expanded to 17.1 times rentals, the variability by city around that median had increased dramatically. Now in some cities the average home was selling at a housing P/E multiple as high as 34.1 whereas in other cities the P/E still hovered at an average of 11.8.

This represents a dramatic change in the way America values its residential real estate. Historically, homes in different cities were essentially valued the same in relation to rents, after allowing for slight pricing differences to account for local weather conditions and amenities, such as restaurants, schools, and job opportunities.

By 2005, all this had changed. Prices of homes in our most highly priced cities relative to rental incomes were worth, on average, many multiples of the same house in a less-costly city. Even after accounting for the fact that rentals are higher in San Francisco than in Albuquerque, homes there still cost three times more when measured by their housing P/E multiple. In other words, housing price differences by city in 2005 could no longer be explained by rental market differences.

This is a very valuable piece of evidence when we seek to uncover the real reason behind the current housing boom. We shall see in chapter 5 that many theories in support of high home prices try to explain why prices have run away in these highest-priced cities, but none of the popular theories adequately explains how prices could have become so out of whack with regard to underlying rentals. In chapters 7, 8, and 9, we try to posit theories of a bubble that do support this home price–rental divergence.

It's also interesting to see which types of cities appear to be the most highly overpriced by this housing multiple approach. The list of the cities with the highest housing P/E multiples in Table 3.1 reads like a lead-in to the television show *Lifestyles of the Rich and Famous*. If high housing P/Es indicate overvalued housing markets, then it appears some of our wealthiest and most successful communities are the most overpriced. Could it be that our wealthiest citizens, who typically are some of our best educated, are naïvely overpaying for the homes in their communities? Maybe the smart people are selling and moving, but it is hard to believe that the new buyers in these wealthy communities are any less well educated. If true, this would be a first: the richest and the best educated are getting the most ripped off. Typically, it is the poor and elderly who suffer the most from confidence schemes.

Or is there a fundamental difference between renting and buying in these wealthy communities that cannot be adequately captured in an economic analysis? I ask this question again in chapter 9. It is difficult to get exactly comparable rental data for the homes that are included in the sales analysis, so some portion of the difference may reflect the fact that renting large prestigious homes is just not an option in some of these very exclusive communities. But that has been a fairly constant problem over time, and therefore does not explain the large housing P/E expansions we have seen in the highest-priced communities. The high-end market for four-bedroom rental properties also exhibits a wide variance in multiples when compared to owned properties.

Just as the last chapter's analysis provided a surprising result as we were able to identify 1981 as the year in which the real current boom began—we reach an equally informative result when we control for rental differences across cities: Our ritziest and wealthiest communities appear to be the most overvalued. This conclusion is an important hint as to a possible explanation of the current boom. The grouping of exclusive communities at the top of the list of the cities with the highest average housing P/E multiples tells us something else: the boom is not random. If, indeed, irrational, unthinking investors are the cause of the bubble, we have to at least give them credit for being organized and deliberate. They didn't just overpay for any property in the country. They overpaid for the best.

Some readers will recall the behavior of the Japanese when they invested in American commercial property in the 1980s: They always insisted on "trophy" properties, regardless of the price they had to pay to close the deal. The tallest office buildings, the best designed, those with the best views caught their eye, and they were willing to pay double or triple the market price in order to complete the acquisition.

At the time, the Japanese were applauded for taking a long-term perspective on their investing, but five years hadn't passed before their overpaying came back to haunt them. Rental incomes fell far short of their monthly costs, and the market would not support any further rent increases. The Japanese real estate venture in America was a bitter experience. They ended up selling almost all of their real estate holdings in America as their company stocks crashed at home. And they typically received for them prices less than half what they had paid.

So, whatever theory we use to explain the housing bubble must also explain why our wealthiest and most exclusive cities have appreciated the most, even relative to rental increases in these towns. This conclusion provides our second great clue to the real cause of the current housing boom. Knowing that wealthy communities have been infected the most with pricing hysteria and that the boom mostly started in 1981 are two important pieces of evidence needed to solve this mystery.

When I was writing my first book on housing prices, the big debate—aside from whether a bubble even existed—was whether the bubble was local or might present a national problem. At the time I argued that it was a national problem. This new data on housing

P/E multiples by city seem to suggest that the boom is indeed local and that any downturn will not have a material national impact.

But I still believe this is wrong. The cities identified here as being the most overvalued relative to their rentals are so large in population and so expensive on a per-property basis that they represent a significant percentage of all residential real estate value in the entire country. The top twenty-two metropolitan markets in terms of housing prices represent more than 40 percent of the aggregate market value of all residential real estate in the country.

Surely, if home prices in these markets fell substantially, the impact would extend to the entire country. Much of the middle of the country has seen appreciation of more like 10 to 30 percent in real housing prices. While this is less than the average appreciation for the coasts, it has occurred in those towns that already house the highest percentage of poor and lower-middle-income residents. It is these people who typically get in trouble when the real estate market tanks, because they do not have cushions of equity or cash to help them make their mortgage payment or make up the shortfall on the sale of an overindebted property. The rich may complain about a real estate downturn, but the foreclosures and personal bankruptcies will appear in the more moderate neighborhoods. And as foreclosures increase, banks have more and more repossessed real estate on their books that they need to get rid of. Thus starts the vicious cycle downward of ever-declining real estate prices.

The second reason the downturn will be national in scope is that the wealthy communities that are the most overvalued are so big that when they collapse, so, too, will the general economy. The real estate business, the mortgage business, the housing construction industry, the home repair and renovation business, and the banks—all will take hits. As the downturn in these key industries works its way through the general economy, there will be layoffs and plant closings. In such economic downturns, the poor and middle class suffer the worst. So a secondary effect of falling prices in the wealthy cities is that jobs will be lost thousands of miles away in the more modest cities and communities. This national economic downturn will of course lead to lower home prices everywhere; the effect will not be limited to the wealthiest cities.

Finally, imagine what will happen to the real estate values in many modest small Florida towns that have shot up from $100,000 to $350,000 if Manhattan's real estate market comes unglued. Many people buying 4,000-square-foot mini mansions in Florida are spending money they "earned" by selling overpriced New York properties. If New York falters, Florida and North Carolina will follow.

In the debate about whether the current housing boom is regional or national in scope, I concede I was wrong: I argued it was national, when it turns out it is international. As the *Economist* magazine pointed out in 2005, the current housing boom is international in scope and is the largest bubble ever. Worldwide, housing values have increased from $40 trillion to over $70 trillion. The $30 trillion increase in value is, incredibly, just about equal to the GDP of the entire advanced world.

Because of the differences in underlying inflation rates in countries around the world it makes sense to look at real housing prices in "world cities" to see if we can uncover any additional clues to the cause of the current boom.

Figure 3.2 is very informative because it gets away from a discussion of growth rates and lets us see what real price levels have done city by city. Again, these are real prices: an adjustment for inflation has already been made. So when we say that prices in New York and London have tripled over the last twenty-five years, this represents a 200 percent real increase in price. We can now ask how their $1.2

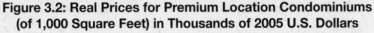

Figure 3.2: Real Prices for Premium Location Condominiums (of 1,000 Square Feet) in Thousands of 2005 U.S. Dollars

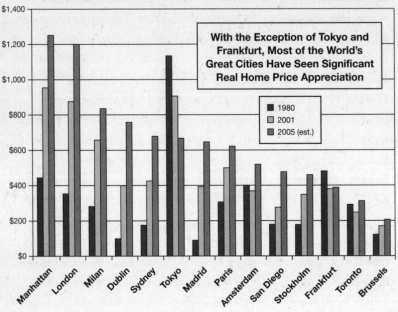

With the Exception of Tokyo and Frankfurt, Most of the World's Great Cities Have Seen Significant Real Home Price Appreciation

- 1980
- 2001
- 2005 (est.)

Source of Data: *The Economist*

million average price condominiums compare in price to similar properties in other cities of the world.

It is difficult when people talk casually about San Diego's housing appreciating at 20 percent per year to make an evaluation of whether this figure is appropriate or not. With this chart, one can see that the recent San Diego appreciation puts it in the middle, based on price, of the great cities of the world. Now, you must still decide whether San Diego *deserves* to be in that company, but at least you are making a real determination based on price and not one based on relative growth rates.

The most dramatic finding of Figure 3.2 is that the housing boom does indeed seem to be international. With the exception of

Tokyo, Frankfurt, and Toronto, the world's great cities have seen dramatic real price increases over the last twenty-five years.

The biggest percentage winners in this group are Dublin and Madrid. Both of these countries had explosive GDP growth over the period as they benefited from the formation of the European Union and opened their borders to foreign investment and trade. Historically, these cities' homes traded at a significant discount of 60 to 80 percent to homes in other European cities such as Amsterdam, Paris, and Milan. Now, from the chart, one can see that Dublin and Madrid have caught these cities in that their homes have just about the same price. The question is no longer the appreciation these cities have experienced in the past, but rather whether they deserve to be valued as highly today as Paris and Milan. And it's not as if Paris and Milan were standing still during these years. Paris prices doubled, and Milan's condominiums tripled in value.

Real estate bulls and bears will interpret this chart quite differently. Bulls will be pleased to see that even after significant run-ups in prices of U.S. real estate, it still seems to trade at a "reasonable" level when compared to housing prices abroad. Bears will be shocked to see that the housing bubble they feared has spread internationally and looks to put the entire world economy at risk.

This is a very important and powerful exhibit in the debate about the cause of the housing boom. Because prices have skyrocketed worldwide, it is much harder to argue that the cause is traceable to circumstances unique to the United States. For example, the popular argument that Mexican immigration, both legal and illegal, is partly responsible for the housing boom in the United States suffers when we look at the international data. Mexican immigration can't be blamed for price increases in Paris, Milan, or London. The fact that housing prices have exploded in many countries of the world and is not uniquely an American phenomenon provides an important clue to a possible explanation for the boom, as we will see in chapters 7, 8, and 9.

Let's look more closely at the winners and losers in Figure 3.2. Home prices have grown tremendously in New York and London while shrinking in Tokyo and Frankfurt. Has there been some fundamental economic shift in these cities that could explain such a dramatic difference in their home values? We know from chapter 1 that Tokyo experienced a dramatic retrenching of its economy and its real estate values over this period. Did its housing just adjust to lower expected economic growth or did it collapse from unsustainable bubble prices? London and New York are benefiting greatly from the global economy, but do their current good fortunes justify that their condo properties trade at three times what Frankfurt sells for or four times what Toronto's cost? Certainly, current incomes in these cities do not justify such a dramatic variance in home values. And even if incomes were higher, why should condos cost more? Shouldn't condo prices reflect their replacement construction costs? It doesn't cost three times as much to add an additional floor to a planned high rise in London compared to Frankfurt.

Figure 3.3 presents a preliminary but revealing analysis of why some international cities have exploded in price recently while others have lagged.

Those cities whose countries experienced the steepest interest rate declines seem to have also witnessed the most rapid appreciation of their residential real estate. This is not a scientific study, but it does suggest that further research might be fruitful. If indeed this turns out to be true, it points to a common cause of the worldwide housing boom. Just as we saw for the United States, many of these countries also began to experience big housing price increases when their nominal interest rates started declining. Unlike the immigration explana-

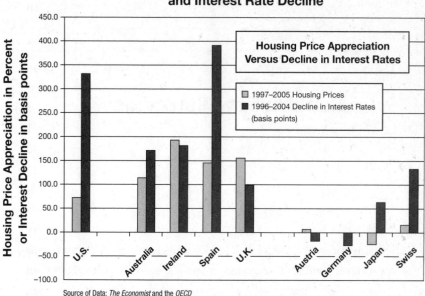

Figure 3.3: International Housing Prices and Interest Rate Decline

Source of Data: *The Economist* and the *OECD*

tion, here we have a possible culprit that may indeed be causing the housing boom, regardless of which country we are discussing.

So the international evidence suggests that the housing boom is not a regional or national phenomenon, but a global problem. And preliminary analysis seems to support the idea that declining nominal interest rates may indeed be part of the problem, not just in the United States, but in many other countries of the world. But just as in the United States, most of the interest rate decline internationally was due to inflation burning out of these economies. This suggests that the change in rates was nominal only and did not dramatically impact real interest rates. If this is so, we still have to explain why home prices might explode upward even though real rates have changed very little. I'll do this in chapter 7, after first exploring some other popular explanations and theories for the boom in chapter 5.

4

Can You Say "Conspiracy"?

Possibly the worst financial advice ever given to the American public was offered by Alan Greenspan in late 2004. Mr. Greenspan touted adjustable-rate mortgages (ARMs) to the public, saying, "American consumers might benefit if lenders provided greater mortgage product alternatives to the traditional fixed-rate mortgage." The most disturbing part of the advice is that we know Greenspan is smart enough to know better. Not only was it terrible advice, but Greenspan must have known it was bad advice before he gave it. Greenspan can be accused of many things, but being dumb is not one of them.

At best, Greenspan had ulterior motives beside simply helping the citizens he was supposed to serve. At worst, he was part of a grand conspiracy to aid the commercial banks and ignore the potential harm to the American public. If so, whose interests was he actually looking out for? Why would the Federal Reserve chairman do something so harmful to his own citizens? Who dreamed up this conspiracy?

At the time of Greenspan's terrible advice, adjustable-rate mortgages were growing tremendously in popularity with the American public. By early 2005, 35 percent of all new mortgages in the country were ARMs, and in California the percentage exceeded 70 percent. In addition to being floating-rate rather than fixed-rate instruments, many of these ARM deals combined other exotic features. Some did not require any principal repayment but rather required only interest payments. Others had initial periods of negative amortization; that is, the principal balance on the loan grew over time rather than declined.

Aggressive commercial banks and mortgage bankers were able to sell these instruments to homebuyers because they argued that it was silly to get a thirty-year fixed-rate mortgage with a higher monthly mortgage payment if the buyer was only going to live in the new home for three to five years. What bankers particularly liked about the new mortgage instruments was that the new floating-rate or interest-only mortgage payment was lower than a standard self-amortizing thirty-year mortgage and so allowed potential homebuyers to qualify for ever-larger amounts of mortgage money. This was important because housing prices had reached such high levels in many communities that average folks could no longer qualify with the banks for the loans needed to buy homes under more conventional mortgage plans.

The homebuyers also bought into the logic. It made sense not to pay a premium to lock in rates for thirty years if they only planned to live in the house for five years. Moreover, experts in real estate, namely the broker and the mortgage banker, were actively pushing the idea. This is why the Fed chairman's comments were so damaging. Surely, the homeowner could trust the chairman of the Federal Reserve to give unbiased advice on the matter. If Greenspan says its good for me to get into ARMs, then it must be so. Isn't that one reason why we have government officials, to give us objective and unbiased expert advice? We look to the Food and Drug Administration to protect us from unsafe drugs. We look to building inspectors to expertly prevent buildings from collapsing, and we should be able to look to the Federal Reserve and the FDIC to expertly protect the banking system from collapsing.

What is so terrible about ARMs that Greenspan knew but didn't tell homebuyers? First of all, long-term thirty-year mortgage rates in 2005 were at a forty-year low. They had peaked at 16.5 percent back in 1981, but by 2005 were around 5.5 percent. This was an excellent opportunity for a homebuyer to lock in a very low rate for thirty years so that the mortgage payments could never vary in the future. If rates went even lower, you could always refinance. It is rare in finance that the public has such a valuable option given to it as the right to refinance if rates decline, but this is typical in thirty-year mortgages. By moving to floating rates, the homebuyer surrendered this option.

But the real travesty in people utilizing ARMs during this period is that it shifted all interest rate risk from the banks to the homeowners. Previously, market interest rates moving was a problem for the commercial banks, which were spending large amounts of money to hedge their interest rate exposure. Under ARM financings, the buyers had volunteered to absorb almost all future interest rate risk. The banks were able to sell the buyer on the idea by offering a short three- or five-year fixed-rate period during which the ARM interest rate did not reset. But after this, the ARM could float, and if market interest rates moved up considerably, then homeowners might see their scheduled monthly mortgage payments increase substantially, say 50 to 70 percent.

It is true that the homebuyer got a slightly lower rate by accepting a floating-rate deal, but because this financing package was being pushed on everyone, home prices immediately increased to offset any benefits resulting from the lower offered initial rate.

The more disturbing part of the story, and the part that Greenspan definitely knew but didn't tell the American public about, is that ARMs don't even make sense for those homebuyers who are only planning to stay put for three or five years. The broker's pitch to them was that they could always sell before the initial ARM's interest rate was scheduled to reset. What they, and Greenspan, forgot to tell the public was that if house prices had declined in the meantime, getting out of the house investment would be extremely difficult. Because trillions of dollars of ARM mortgages had been sold, there are literally tens of millions of households that will be in big trouble if interest rates increase in the near future and housing prices decline.

No one wanting to sell a home likes to see a down market for home prices. But the problem is multiplied for the ARM-financed homeowner. A homeowner with fixed-rate long-term debt has a locked-in monthly mortgage payment that cannot change in the future. If he doesn't like the housing market, he can always decide not to sell his home and continue to live in it and make his monthly mortgage payments. The ARM's homeowner has no such choice. Even if he believes a downturn in home prices might be temporary, he will be forced to sell his house into a weak market. The reason is that his mortgage payments will jump as soon as his initial fixed-rate period has expired if interest rates have increased. He will be between a rock and a hard place—declining market values for his home and increasing monthly mortgage payments.

And here is the real dilemma. He is not alone. Tens of millions of ARM households may face the same decision—sell into a down market or try to find a way to afford a much larger mortgage payment. Because so many will face this quandary at the same time, housing prices will grow even softer. Many people will sell into a weak housing market, not because they want to, but because they have to in order to avoid their ever-increasing mortgage payments. Such a selling stampede will drive housing prices even lower. And then the real carnage begins. Once housing prices are off 20 to 30 percent in some areas, many ARM homeowners will be financially underwater; that is, a home will be worth less in the market than the balance on the mortgage. And when that happens, the way out is not to sell but to allow the bank to foreclose and take possession of the home. Banks, too, will then begin selling repossessed real estate into the down market, joining the legion of ARM holders needing to sell and however many fixed-rate homeowners who have lost confidence in the housing market.

This is not idle speculation. More than $1 trillion of ARM mortgages are due to reset in 2007. And because interest rates are so low, their allowable increase in rate is a very large percentage of their total mortgage cost. Monthly payments could easily increase 50 to 70 percent. So the people who utilized ARM financings in order to stretch to afford their homes are exactly the ones who will suffer the greatest increases in rate. If you didn't qualify to buy a home utilizing a fixed-rate mortgage at 5.5 percent in 2005, you are not going to be able to afford to keep it when ARMs reset to 7 or 9 percent.

This is not a simple story, and the complexity is part of the reason so many homebuyers fell for the ARM pitch from their bankers. But there is one person in this country who must have known the full story back in 2004. That man is Alan Greenspan. We can argue about why he said what he did, but there is no question that Greenspan must have known the ramifications of his bad advice even before he gave it.

Why then would Greenspan purposely give bad advice to the people he has sworn to protect and serve? No man can serve two masters. For the answer to this question we need to digress for a moment to discover where Greenspan's true loyalties lie.

Each quarter, Greenspan appears before Congress or issues a publicly available press release to comment on how he sees the American economy performing and what he has done to fight inflation, the Fed chairman's primary responsibility. Without exception, every time he has made such a report he has said, or implied, that he once again has been successful in quelling inflation for another quarter, and how, by keeping wages down.

Whose wages do you think he is talking about? We have seen economic growth and worker productivity increase greatly during his tenure, but almost no real increase in American wages. Greenspan is correct that part of his job is to help control inflation, but it should be limited to controlling the printing of new money which is what drives general inflation. By interfering in the wage-setting process of the free market for labor, he has become an enormously destructive force to American labor, and it has suffered greatly as a result.

So, again we face the same question. Why would Greenspan interfere in the markets to harm the average American worker? To see the answer clearly you must understand who Greenspan really works for.

It is true that the Federal Reserve chairman is appointed by the president, but the twelve regional Federal Reserve banks are controlled by our nation's commercial banks. Each reserve bank is managed by a board of nine directors, six of whom are nominated to serve by our commercial banks. And if you want to understand how they will decide any issue just ask one simple question, what is in the commercial banks' best interests?

On many issues, what is good for the banking industry is good for Americans. But sometimes American workers' interests diverge from the banks', and it unfortunate that the Federal Reserve chairman under those circumstances always seems to side with his banking friends. Keeping American wages low, under the guise of fighting inflation, is one of those cases where Greenspan clearly puts the interest of his banking friends above the American worker. By keeping wages down, he helps American corporations become more profitable, and thus makes the bank's corporate lending portfolio all the more secure and profitable. To Greenspan, it is an unfortunate side effect that the American worker suffers so.

When it comes to housing and Greenspan's unforgivable bad advice on ARMs, it all becomes much clearer when one understands that Greenspan's primary allegiance is to the commercial banks and not to the public. By suggesting that Americans should take advantage of ARM financings, Greenspan should have recognized that he was harming American homebuyers. He was helping shift a potentially enormous problem from the commercial banks to the shoulders of the average workingman. In one piece of terrible advice, Greenspan was able to shift substantial future interest rate risk from his commercial banks and their balance sheets to American homeowners. He just forgot to disclose that he wasn't working on behalf of the American people, he was working to protect his banking cronies and prevent a possible future problem with the American banking system. Of course, the increasing utilization of ARM financings in the housing business has not reduced the risk to the banking system, it has worsened it. Shifting risk to individual homeowners does not free the banks from the credit risk they face of mortgage defaults, personal bankruptcies, and foreclosures.

And this is a criticism that will linger long after Greenspan retires from the Fed. He has often been characterized as taking the expedient easy road rather than fighting for any fundamental change in how business is conducted. It was Greenspan who started this whole real estate bubble mess when he cut interest rates to 1 percent to try to prevent the dot.com bubble from dragging the entire economy down with it when it burst. Greenspan knew about that bubble also, but rather than doing anything substantive about it he just made a statement about "irrational exuberance" in 1997, and then went about his business. He has been even more irresponsible during the housing boom by refusing to use the word "bubble" or admit that it is a national, and even international, problem. Rather, he insists on labeling it merely a regional problem in a few select cities subject to some "frothiness" in house prices.

Root beers are frothy. He only made the soft comment on frothiness so that if the market disintegrates before he retires, he can claim he made some statement on the record. He does little to supervise his fellow bankers, whose overaggressiveness is one of the real reasons we are in the mess to begin with. We shall see in chapter 7 that the banks are the number-one suspect as the real culprit behind this housing bubble, but Greenspan is the last person who will ever point an accusatory finger at his banking associates.

Greenspan, and the Bush administration, make a second fundamental error in handling the housing boom. In addition to the leniency they have shown the commercial banks, they operate from a neoconservative, pro-business perspective that fails to appreciate that the government has a proper role in supervising markets. They do not see that without government rules regarding property and contractual rights, there would be no effective markets. Their enthusiasm for free markets arises from a political tradition that seeks to constrain all government regulation of banking and industry. A great many people have forgotten that there is such a thing as good and necessary regulation of business and markets. If the housing and mortgage markets collapse, they will be served a rude reminder.

It was these same neocon free marketers who supported the privatization of the Russian economy in the 1990s without first establishing the rule of law and an independent judiciary, thus causing corruption to explode as a new class of oligarchs was created.

It is not just economic philosophy that drives Greenspan and the Bush administration to avoid the proper regulation of the banking sector and the mortgage industry. This administration has been corrupted by a system that allows our biggest banks and corporations to "buy off" our elected representatives through campaign contributions and lobbying efforts. Once the housing market collapses we will all wonder why nothing was done sooner to prevent it. The answer of course is that most of our elected representatives in both parties, including our president, were being given a great deal of money not to do their jobs and not to protect the American people.

This pay for service is rampant throughout the federal government, but quite possibly the most damaging example is the way we regulate Fannie Mae and Freddie Mac. It was obvious to me when I wrote my first book in 2003 that these companies were too highly leveraged with debt and that too many of their business decisions were driven by an attempt to enrich their managements through profit-sharing schemes and generous stock options. Now, after they have announced tens of billions of dollars in unanticipated accounting adjustments and replaced their senior managements, they still are not receiving the government supervision they should. These two behemoths of the mortgage industry sit on trillions of dollars' worth of mortgages, and yet Congress has been very slow to properly regulate them. They enjoy an implied guarantee from the American taxpayer that saves them millions in borrowing costs, and yet they feel no need to be regulated by Congress. It is the corruption of their multimillion-dollar lobbying effort that assures that congressmen look the other way, even after there has been every indication that there is a very serious problem. It would be sad enough if Fannie and Freddie were a major cause of a housing fiasco in the future that ended up harming many American families. It is inexcusable that our Congress has failed to act to better regulate these quasi agencies having had the warnings that we have seen to date.

One final concern with Greenspan and our regulators of the mortgage industry. They have adopted a paternalistic attitude where they think they know what is best for the American people, and therefore are quite comfortable conducting their business in relative secrecy. They feel no need to report honestly to the public on meetings they have held with industry participants.

Fannie Mae had meetings with the biggest players in the homebuilding industry in 2005 to warn them about the damaging impact of interest-only mortgages, but never felt compelled to warn the American public. As of this writing, they still have not disclosed the transcripts from that meeting.

The FDIC has similarly met with its member banks to caution them about overly aggressive lending practices in an attempt to get them to curtail the use of exotic mortgage instruments, but no details have emerged as to exactly what was said. Does it make sense that the biggest banks and companies in the homebuilding industry are warned about potential problems that may have serious repercussions on the price of homes and yet no warning or alert is given to the public? Telling the public there is no such thing as a national bubble while warning big industrial participants to limit their exposure to aggressive lending practices reminds one of Wall Street during the Internet bubble. Research analysts were actively promoting and recommending stocks to the public while at the same time advising their own firms to limit their exposure to these stocks. While completely illegal on Wall Street, the grievance here seems much worse, since government officials are supposed to act in the public's best interest. Not only are the Federal Reserve and officials of the FDIC acting dishonestly and fraudulently, they are violating the oath they made to protect and serve the American public and honor the Constitution.

You don't have to believe in a grand conspiracy in order to realize that there is a housing bubble. But to those of you who depend on the government to protect your interests, you should be aware that times have changed. Your government is now controlled by the nation's biggest banks and corporations, which contribute to the election campaigns of elected officials and lobby them daily. Our government's allegiance has shifted from concern for the people's business to profiting from it and allying themselves with big business. The housing crash will provide the evidence that people will point to in order to demonstrate with certainty that our government no longer puts your best interests at heart. It is sad that such pain to average Americans has to occur before people will act to reform our unrepresentative government, but Americans are slow to act, often doing nothing until after disasters explode.

In August 2005, Greenspan took the opportunity to hedge his optimistic views on housing. Just as during the dot.com bubble when he spoke of "irrational exuberance" and then did nothing to contain rabid speculation in the market, so, too, is he now trying to go on record as having at least expressed caution about high home prices. One, it is a bit late. Two, he hasn't acted on his words in any meaningful way, and three, he delivered his warning in typical unintelligible Greenspan-speak. Here is what he said: "This vast increase in the market value of asset claims [house prices] is in part the indirect result of investors accepting lower compensation for risk. Such an increase in market value is too often viewed by market participants as structural and permanent. . . . history has not dealt kindly with the aftermath of protracted periods of low-risk premiums."

It will be left to future generations to sort through the Federal Reserve chairman's tens of thousands of pages of speeches and testimony to Congress. If in reading this passage, Greenspan is given any credit for warning us about the impending danger of a housing crash, then he will have succeeded in protecting his legacy. I believe history will judge Greenspan and the current Congress and this administration much more harshly as caring much too deeply about bank and corporate profitability and knowingly creating an unsustainable housing bubble that threatened our very republic when it crashed. Everyone will certainly comprehend then that American homeowners took a beating during a housing crash that was the result of an unsustainable boom orchestrated and propped up by their government and big business, who were more interested in corporate profits than in the welfare of their fellow citizens.

5

Why Eight Popular Theories Fail
to Explain the Boom

There are various theories bandied about in the media as to what is really causing home prices to increase. The majority are advanced by real estate industry representatives in an attempt to convince home-buyers that the prices they are seeing are completely rational and easily explained and that, therefore, no one should worry about the price stability of the market going forward. The thinking is that if a reasonable explanation can be presented for why home prices are astronomically high, then maybe they will remain there or increase in the future and thus encourage buyers not to delay their purchases.

The problem with almost all of these armchair empiricists is that they make no attempt to tie their explanations of rising prices to the evidence observed in the market. A thorough explanation would require a statistical analysis to see whether there is indeed a correlation between the causes they present and actual home price movements. Even without a thorough statistical analysis it is easy to demonstrate whether their predictive theories fit what we know about housing prices.

While there are millions of pieces of data available on housing prices, a reasonable test of any proposed theory is whether it explains the pricing evidence presented in chapters 2 and 3. Namely, any theory supporting price escalation must be consistent with the following three empirical findings:

1. Real U.S. home prices have been relatively flat for the last hundred years and only since 1981 have doubled in real terms.
2. The wealthiest cities and neighborhoods have seen the greatest home price appreciation recently, and these price increases have far outstripped rental growth in these exclusive markets.
3. The recent housing boom has not been limited to the United States but has been in full swing worldwide, as evidenced in countries such as Britain, Ireland, Spain, Australia, and France.

A theory is not much good if it doesn't fit the data, and here we have a broad range of evidence across history and the world and even across individual cities and towns. Just because a theory sounds plausible, it will never gain credence until it can accurately fit the data. This is a requirement of any theory that pretends to be predictive. It must at a minimum explain the historical data available.

Theory 1: Supply and Demand Drive Housing Prices

It is hard to argue with this general statement and not draw the wrath of every economist on the planet. Supply and demand is the foundation of pricing in every free market. In the short run, it is true. Supply and demand do indeed cause pricing movements in perfect markets. The problem is that supply and demand have a way of changing fairly quickly over time: The supply of homes for sale may be tight today; it might not be tomorrow. Many pundits mistakenly assume we are talking about the supply of newly constructed homes and conclude that these couldn't be built quickly and brought on the market to meet demand. But this isn't what "supply" means to a market economist. The supply of homes for sale at any time on a market is not solely dependent on new construction. Every day, current homeowners make a conscious decision whether to sell their homes or not. The supply of homes available for sale at any time can change dramatically without any newly built homes coming on the market. If prices hypothetically drop 10 percent in a market, the price decline may bring out a horde of new sellers who had delayed selling in an attempt to catch the peak. Or if prices increase 10 percent more, classic supply curve thinking predicts there will be many more sellers who will find this new higher price too attractive to pass up.

Therefore, any supply and demand arguments that real estate professionals make about the strength of the housing market by citing statistics on the volume of sales or inventory of homes for sale on the market should be met with a great deal of skepticism. These statistics can turn very quickly in a down market, so fast that taking advantage of the turn in prices is nearly impossible. For example, the inventory of homes for sale may currently be at 4.5 months of average sales volume, but when the market turns, this number could increase quickly. If monthly sales volumes halve and inventory doubles, this ratio could very quickly increase to 16 months or more. More likely, if the market softens, many optimistic sellers will pull their properties off the market hoping that the downturn is temporary. If that occurs it will artificially deflate this statistic at a time you wish you had sold.

Think of how individual stocks are priced in the stock market. Traders sitting on the trading floor react almost exclusively to supply and demand considerations minute by minute to set prices. But that supply and demand is being created by research staffs and the analysis of investors who are taking a much longer time frame into account in their calculation of a company's future earnings prospects. The trader only sees this minute's supply and demand, but a great deal of longer-term value thinking goes into creating those market forces. And if the fundamental reasons for a stock's attractiveness change, then those supply and demand forces can change quickly and quite violently.

Supply and demand can change so fast to reflect new information on a change in fundamentals that at times it appears that prices change with no increased buying and selling. Academic studies have found that share prices of target companies reacted within 90 seconds to merger announcements, sometimes with very few changes in share volume. The same thing can happen to the housing market. You don't need an increase in the number of sellers necessarily to see a price decline. If there is a shift in the fundamentals driving housing prices, such as a rise in interest rates or a decline in the economy, housing prices can decline almost instantaneously with very few actual sales. All that has to happen is for the prospective buyers and sellers to agree that the change in fundamentals has negatively affected housing prices. If both prospective buyers and prospective sellers wake up and honestly believe housing prices should be 10 percent lower in a particular market, they could head that much lower without a single actual sale. Sales are just hard evidence of what the market already knows; homes under this scenario are not worth now what they were worth previously.

In addition, the housing and mortgage markets are not perfect markets. I find them to be incredibly incestuous, with real estate agents who don't necessarily represent your interests, appraisers who are paid to justify high prices, and banks that often lend 100 percent of the purchase price but hold few of the mortgage loans they create. Fannie Mae and Freddie Mac act like for-profit companies when it comes to paying their executives, but enjoy an implied guarantee from the federal government. Our government should be regulating all of this, but has been paid by big campaign contributors to stand down and let the market take care of any problems that result.

If the housing market is not a perfect market, then any arguments about supply and demand properly determining prices are probably just plain wrong. What incentive do buyers have to limit the prices they pay for properties if none of the money is coming out of their pocket? Increasingly, many of the buyers of investment properties in Florida are foreigners, especially Europeans enjoying the premium that the euro has enjoyed relative to the U.S. dollar. How is a bank ever going to get to these foreign buyers if the market tanks and foreclosed property sales are not adequate to cover mortgage amounts?

A twist on the supply and demand argument is that housing prices cannot decline in the future because sellers need a place to live. Unlike stocks which people can sell, people live in their homes. It is mistakenly argued that because people need a place to live, they can't easily put their houses on the market to sell. But, people can always sell and rent if they feel prices are abnormally high. People can also sell and move to a less expensive city or town. No such selling action has to occur to have real price declines. As we said above, buyers and sellers may reach an entirely new understanding that home prices are overvalued and need to adjust downward with very few actual sales. It is not the one or two sellers in a town that drive the price of all the homes in the community lower. Rather, all buyers and sellers pretty much agree that fundamentals like interest rates and the economy have caused all homes to be worth less. You just don't see it until one or two properties actually change hands. They are not the cause of the decline, they are the result.

So be very wary if a person with little economics training starts throwing around supply and demand as the reason that the housing market is properly valued.

Theory 2: Home Prices Have Always Gone Up

Not only is this an argument offered by aggressive brokers as to why one should not worry about currently high real estate prices, but buyers act on the advice and pay prices that cannot be sustained without further expected price increases in the future. It's clear that the prices being paid for condominiums in Miami and San Diego only make sense if prices continue to rise at a fairly fast rate. If prices just level off with no decline, many of these condo purchases would be in real trouble. Even in this low interest rate environment, monthly carrying costs are quite negative on these properties, and that assumes that they can be successfully rented. If they become vacant due to oversupply and lack of rental demand, the carrying costs turn much worse.

These buyers are making a classic mistake in their purchase analysis. They are assuming because prices have gone up in the past they will continue to go up in the future. But as we showed in chapter 1, you can't just draw a trend line through historical prices to get a prediction of future prices. Such an assumption violates a basic arbitrage condition that marketable assets shouldn't appreciate faster than the general inflation rate or else people could buy today and sell tomorrow and make a risk-free profit. For most markets, today's price is the best predictor of tomorrow's future price, possibly with some small allowance for growth equal to general inflation.

This can be seen most clearly by looking at Shiller's hundred-year graph of housing prices in chapter 2. Is it more likely that housing prices will continue to trend ever higher as they have since 1981, or return to some historical norm?

Certainly, this idea that trees grow to the sky violates the experience elsewhere in the world. Japan's housing market experienced growth like ours in the 1980s and then reversed and gave up almost all of its gains. Australia has been in a housing boom for years, but prices in Sydney dropped some 16 percent in one quarter in 2005. Britain's housing boom was longer and steeper than that in the United States, and yet as interest rates have increased prices there have begun to stabilize or decline.

The striking thing about the evidence presented in chapters 2 and 3 is that much of this housing price data is in real terms; that is, it has been adjusted for inflation. So 100 percent increases in real home prices for the United States and 200 percent real increases for New York, London, and other international cities over time are huge. Everyone was accustomed to double-digit growth rates back when inflation was 10 to 15 percent. But in the brave new world of 2 to 3 percent inflation, it is hard to imagine how rents and salaries will grow fast enough to support these extraordinary housing price increases. That is why the separation of housing prices and rents is so important. It is one way of showing that home prices cannot escape the fundamental forces that drive them in the long term, namely, rents and incomes. If rents and the economy grow at 3 percent a year, and housing prices continue to grow at 10 to 15 percent per year, not only will the bubble grow exponentially, but people will be asked to pay an even larger portion of their paycheck toward their housing costs. With both parents working and 40 percent-plus of their salaries currently targeted toward paying the mortgage, how much more can they pay? And that assumes interest rates stay stable and low.

Theory 3: The Baby Boom,
Immigration, and Population Growth Fuel House Prices

Probably the most popular reason cited by real estate industry insiders as to why housing prices will continue to escalate is the increased demand from baby boomers and immigrants.

But this argument fails to meet any of our three empirical tests. It doesn't explain why other countries are experiencing a housing boom. It doesn't explain why real housing prices were flat previously. (Didn't the sellers know previously about immigration and the baby boom?) And it doesn't explain why our largest and wealthiest communities are experiencing the greatest price increases without a commensurate increase in rental prices.

But it remains a popular explanation for the current boom. It is easy to dismiss immigration as an important cause of the current bubble in real estate prices. Most new immigrants to our country are poor, mostly from Mexico, and could not possibly be responsible for the increase in prices seen in our wealthiest communities. Most of these poor immigrants are renters, so if they had any impact they should drive rents up relative to housing prices, and that is just the opposite of what we see in the data. Immigration did not just start in the recent past when the real prices of homes began their escalation. Immigration had been going full swing for decades before this. And our international data suggest that many foreign countries are experiencing housing booms of their own without significant numbers of new immigrants.

When immigration is included in a sophisticated statistical analysis of housing prices across the country it fails to explain any of the increase in prices that has occurred. The easiest way to see this is to realize that Texas has seen almost no housing price appreciation recently and yet has a very large Mexican immigration. San Antonio, which has the largest influx of Mexican immigrants of any major city in the country, has witnessed a real decline in housing prices of nearly 20 percent over the last decade.

The baby boom gets blamed for many things by economists, but if boomers are the ones overpaying for housing, they haven't learned much over the years. Pundits quickly point out that baby boomers are purchasing second homes to use as vacation and retirement homes, but fail to mention that the fastest price appreciation is in our biggest cities, not near our rivers and streams and vacation hideaways.

If baby boomers are getting ready to retire, and are scared that the prices of retirement homes are escalating so fast that they may miss the opportunity to buy, they may be doing themselves a great injustice by hurrying to the market. Home prices in retirement communities can temporarily escalate, reflecting increased demand, but all that is needed is time for builders to construct new homes and meet the temporary excess demand. If there is no land shortage in these retirement communities, one can be certain that prices will eventually head back to a better approximation of building costs. And even if land becomes scarce and valuable, the high rise building craze in Miami, Las Vegas, and San Diego demonstrates that you can always build up rather than out to deal with land scarcity.

Prices have increased in many cities like Mumbai in India and Shanghai in China without the aid of any baby boom. Neither India nor China had any post–World War II baby boom to speak of.

Another common argument about the baby boom and house prices is that the boomers' children are now of an age when they are looking for their first homes, and this increased demand is driving home prices ever higher. Of course, the industry experts that make this argument forget to mention that these same baby boomers have parents that are either very old and facing death or have moved into nursing homes and assisted living centers, freeing up millions of housing properties. Even if a child inherits the property and decides to live in the house rather than sell it, this is one less person in the market for a new home. Some 22 million homes in the United States, approximately 20 percent of the entire country's housing stock, are owned by people 65 years of age or older.

There does appear to be an unusual number of warm-weather coastal towns that have witnessed significant real price appreciation lately. If it is being caused by the retiring baby boomers, then be careful, for it may not last. The argument that there is only a limited supply of coastline is rather felicitous. The coastline has not gotten any shorter over the last decade as prices have escalated. Prices have escalated in many backwater Florida towns for inferior homes that are going to be have to be torn down before any real vacation homes can be constructed. There is nothing unique about having a home in humid and hot rural inland Florida that a homebuilding company could not duplicate by building a new home for $100,000, if you only give it a couple of years to catch up to the surprising demand.

Theory 4: Tax Benefits Make It Cheaper to Own Than Rent

Many homebuyers immediately conclude that because they get to deduct mortgage interest from their taxable income, owning a home is always less expensive than renting a similar property. They approach the analysis as if all the other variables are constant. They are not. Today the price of homes moves quite independently of the rental market, and in some of our largest cities is completely disconnected from it.

It is true that the tax deductibility of mortgage interest has real economic value, but it is also true that this value declines as nominal interest rates decline as inflation eases. As we have seen, in the mideighties, the tax deduction might have represented as much as 30 percent of the value that one paid for a property; today it is more like 9 percent.

The key to seeing if this deduction creates value for homeowners is determining whether they paid for it up front when they purchased the home. If the price of the home is simply increased by the value of the tax deduction, then there is absolutely no value from the tax deduction that accrues to an owner rather than a renter. In effect, when people sell homes they sell the physical asset, the house, but also a stream of future tax savings which gets present-valued and included in the purchase price.

Here is an example with numbers. Suppose you purchase a home for $1 million. Let's finance it with a 6 percent thirty-year fixed-rate mortgage. This means that the interest portion of your mortgage payment is going to be approximately $5,000 per month. This might seem a bit high, but you probably couldn't find a comparable rental for this price that is as nice in the same neighborhood. And besides, your after-tax interest-only cost is more like $3,500 per month.

But this is not anywhere near your total cost of ownership. As any homeowner knows, there will be significant closing costs. If we assume you hold the property for ten years and your total costs going in and out are 5 percent each way, then one can amortize this total cost and recognize an additional monthly cost of $830 per month. Property taxes vary by city, but let's assume for these purposes they are 1 percent per year, or another $830 per month. Maintenance expenses can run 1.5 percent per year, and probably more like 2.5 percent per year if you include necessary larger home repair projects as well as renovations (Many condominium organizations in New York City charge 3 to 4 percent per year in maintenance fees and do no work to the interior of the apartments.) This is another $2,080 per month in costs. So we have total occupation costs per month of $8,740 pretax, or $7,240 after-tax.

Now it is fairly obvious that at these monthly costs our total occupation charges from owning may indeed exceed our rental costs. It is hard to imagine not being able to find a comparable property at these rent levels. Because the average apartment in New York is now priced above $1 million, all we would need to do is find an "average" one- or two-bedroom apartment at a price less than these monthly costs and we would be ahead of the game.

This analysis leaves out one very important variable: how much housing prices are going to increase in the future in real terms. I say real terms, because if it just keeps up with general inflation you have not earned any extra spending money, because everything will be higher in price by that same amount. Most economists believe that today's real price is the best predictor of tomorrow's real price. You would be radical, at least judged by economists, if you thought housing was going to increase 1 percent per year in the future in real terms. As a matter of fact, because home prices are perceived by many to be currently overvalued, some economists are predicting that home prices might decline as much as 10 to 15 percent per year for the next three or four years.

This variable alone is large enough to swamp all the prior analysis. If home prices increase 2 to 3 percent more per year in real terms for the next ten years this might be enough to justify paying today's prices rather than renting.

But many buyers' expectations of real price increases in the future are totally unrealistic. Surveys indicate that many buyers expect double-digit annual home price increases to continue for many years into the future. And as we have seen, if that is the basis of your bid for a property, you are going to be in big trouble if those price increases fail to materialize. If you are holding the property as an investment, and have negative carrying costs, you may have to hold it for a much longer time than you anticipated to reach breakeven, assuming the property ever gets to breakeven.

There is no economic reason to think that owning is always less expensive than renting regardless of how many tax benefits follow from ownership.

Theory 5: Housing Can't Go Down
as Long as the Economy Remains Strong

It is typically a weak economy that is the undoing of a real estate bubble. The reason is that until jobs are lost, people always manage to muddle through and find a way to make their mortgage payment.

The U.S. economy has been growing at a real rate of approximately 3.5 percent, or given its 1 percent population growth, a per capita increase of 2.5 percent per year. This normally would be considered very healthy for an advanced economy, especially given that Japan is still struggling with near-zero real growth and Germany and France are having trouble getting more than 2 percent per year in growth.

But there are unusual circumstances to the U.S. economic numbers these days. Economists are having trouble understanding why more new jobs are not being created. And while unemployment seems moderate, there are a vast number of Americans who are choosing to cease employment rather than continue to work. Take away the housing boom and we have had no real economic growth since 2000. In fact, without the housing bubble, the country would have been in a deep and long recession for the last six years.

As we've seen in chapter 4, the housing bubble was not some random mistake that fell upon us. Rather, it was the Fed's solution to getting us out from under the dot.com collapse without worsening the recession. The Fed knew that creating a bubble in housing was incredibly stimulative to the economy, but at the time they thought they had no choice.

While it is impressive that the economy is shrugging off high oil prices, the truth of the matter is that America is no longer a manufacturing powerhouse. Only 10 percent of our workers have jobs in manufacturing. China and the developing world are the world's manufacturing engines now, and I believe that much of the productivity improvements credited to American workers actually today trace back to the effort of the workers in these developing countries.

The real reason that the American economy is maintaining its growth record is twofold—spending on housing and the military. Military and increased government deficit spending are acting just as Keynes predicted they would, as pumps to the demand side of the economy. By the time all the military and intelligence spending is added up, including the spending of new departments like Homeland Security, nearly half of all government spending is accounted for by military and defense. This, in combination with a $4 trillion tax cut, is enormously stimulative to the economy.

Housing's stimulative impact on the economy is much easier to understand. Without the boom in housing prices, you can cut the number of real estate brokers and mortgage bankers in half, if not more. You can probably draw a line through half of the commercial banks' profitability. Forget home improvement sales, as renovation would cease if people ever thought their $500,000 home they bought was really only worth $320,000. And the biggest impact of all: new construction would virtually cease. Without new construction, I don't know what many people would do for work in this country, especially many illegal aliens who have become an informal painting and construction force of their own.

I think that alone accounts for all of the supposed growth in our economy, but there are two other important effects of the boom. First, because people believe their houses have doubled in value, they are feeling wealthier and are willing to buy a lot of other goods and services. Beyond this psychological effect, mortgage refinancings have provided billions of dollars to homeowners to use for additional extravagant purchases outside their homes.

Second, while consumption has increased, more than 100 percent of this increased buying has been funded with debt, mostly new mortgage debt. Economists argue that people's equity has increased as well, but most of this increase is due to home price increases. Take away the appreciation in the price of homes and you are left with current consumption financed with long-term debt, always a recipe for disaster.

This then is the real danger of the current housing bubble and why some of us are taking it so seriously. Unlike the stock market bubble that was financial in origin, the housing bubble is based on assets that many of us hold and build or manage for a living. The real danger is that at the time the housing bubble is deflating, the real economy will find out it sorely misses its housing component. Just as our housing asset values readjust downward, our economy will tank. As the economy declines, more and more Americans will have trouble paying their mortgages. And behind all of it is the fact that 80 to 100 percent of the price of these overinflated assets has been funded by our commercial banks, the lifeblood of our productive economy. One cannot paint a gloomy enough picture of the economic problems associated with a steep decline in housing prices. Never assume our economy is so strong we needn't worry about it.

Theory 6: Escalating
Construction Costs Cause Home Price Increases

This is a common argument that is used to explain ever-increasing housing prices. Unfortunately, while it may have been true decades ago, it is no longer the case.

Edward Glaeser, Joe Gyourko, and Raven Saks have recently written an informative research paper entitled "Why Have Housing Prices Gone Up?" for the *American Economic Review* that dispels the notion that housing prices have increased recently because building costs are increasing. The authors find that increases in building and construction costs do not explain the recent run-up in housing. Their analysis is dead-on, and because it is impossible to improve upon I will only attempt to summarize their work here.

The authors agree that, recently, home prices are appreciating fastest in the most expensive cities. Prior to 1970, they found that home price increases nationally were almost totally explained by higher construction costs and the fact that houses were growing larger with greater amenities attached to them. In the 1970s, the world started to change. Certain coastal cities like Los Angeles, San Francisco, and San Diego began to have home price increases that were not fully explainable by increases in construction costs.

In the 1980s, this pricing trend spread to interior regions of California such as Sacramento and to the Northeast Corridor, from New York City to Boston. In these areas, building or construction costs represented less than 60 percent of the total price of a home. Either the home was overvalued relative to construction costs, the land underlying was increasing rapidly in value, or something, such as local regulations, was restricting builders from constructing new homes in these areas. The authors' presumption is that if homebuilders were able to build new homes more cheaply than the price that homes sold for in the market, they would. This new building, if allowed under zoning rules, would stabilize home prices in the area.

By 2000, the unexplained contagion of higher home prices had spread to twenty-seven metropolitan areas in which the physical house and its cost of construction could account for, at most, 60 percent of the total home price. Cities such as Ann Arbor, Austin, Denver, and Nashville had been added to the list of cities with unexplained housing price increases, or at least unexplained by physical building construction costs. By 2000, building structure accounted for less than 30 percent of the total purchase price in the country's highest-priced markets, mostly on the two coasts.

For example, the authors point out that between 1970 and 2000, real construction costs of houses in San Francisco increased 4.6 percent, in total, while real home prices in San Francisco increased by 270 percent over the same period. The story is not too different for Boston where construction costs increased 6.6 percent, in total, from 1970 to 2000, and yet home prices there increased 127 percent during the period.

The authors find that real construction costs of a modest-quality one-story home have not grown at all nationwide, on average, since 1970. In constant 2000 dollars, the cost of construction of such a home was $63,600 in 1970 and by 2000 had declined to $61,600. While these numbers are reported after accounting for general inflation, the fact that the real price went down must mean that the construction industry has witnessed cost savings due to increases in labor productivity or decreases in their general raw material costs. Certainly there was plenty of demand for the finished houses.

This extremely thorough analysis by these authors presents very strong evidence that the recent increase in home prices is not due to increasing building and construction costs. We will return in chapter 6 to the question, If not building costs, then what? It seems that either the supply of new homes is being constrained by zoning restrictions, land has gotten awfully expensive, demand is up because of a newfound desire on behalf of people to be homeowners, easy money and poorly regulated markets are driving the growth in home prices, or maybe just everybody is acting irrationally and there is no logical explanation for the housing bubble. We will examine each of these possible explanations in later chapters.

Theory 7: Homebuilders'
Stock Prices Show the Housing Market Is on Solid Ground

Prognosticators on television and in the print media often make the mistake of confusing the health of homebuilding companies with the overall stability of prices in housing. What they fail to realize is that homebuilders are typically sellers of houses, not buyers. Homebuilders like overpriced housing markets. That is how they make their money. They take nails and wood and turn them into overpriced houses that they then sell to the public. The higher the home prices the better, even if the prices have no semblance of reality.

Homebuilders can be thought of as arbitragers who are trying to correct overvalued markets by introducing new supply to the market. As prices get high in a particular area, whether it is rational or irrational demand that is driving the price increase, the homebuilders are motivated to step in and build. That is what they do. The proper working of the construction market creates a profit-making opportunity by the uptick in home prices, and it continues until enough new construction is completed to meet demand.

So homebuilders are not betting that high home prices will continue; they are doing their level best to prevent them from escalating. It is as if Ferraris started to appreciate in value and the company was able to turn out more cars to satisfy the demand and maintain current price levels.

Many homebuilders are not mere sellers of houses. They may limit their risk to a housing downturn even further by preselling many of the houses they build. Even a seller of real estate can get burned in an overpriced market if the market collapses before the seller has time to close on the property. The problem is complicated for the homebuilders who historically built many of their houses on speculation and did not get paid until they sold them after completion of construction. No longer willing to take that risk in an overly inflated market, many homebuilders are now preselling their homes, often before ground is even broken to begin building. They get paid the agreed-upon price even if the housing market crashes. The risk of a decline in the housing market under such a scheme is squarely on the shoulders of the buyer, not the homebuilder.

So even though homebuilders are on the sell side of the market, and have found a way to eliminate a great deal of the risk of a housing collapse from their business, it is still informative to look at their stock market valuations as this is the market's best measure of how housing market participants are faring.

As expected, their earnings have exploded recently. I say, as expected, because they have been net sellers into an extremely hot and rapidly rising market. But these exorbitant earnings of the homebuilders tell us something more. If increased home prices were solely due to rational and real increases in the costs of doing business, such as higher land costs or more difficult zoning regulations, we would not expect to see such dramatic growth in the profitability of the entire homebuilding industry. These excessive profits hint at the fact that there is something else going on here beyond simple supply constraints. People are paying big prices for homes, but it's not due to higher construction costs. And because the builders are making so much money the profits must be due to more than just increased land appreciation or zoning restriction costs. This is the best evidence we have uncovered yet that something is going on with the demand side of the equation that at first blush looks a bit irrational. We will return to this discussion in chapter 8.

The other interesting thing we can learn from examining the stock prices of the homebuilders is that, somewhat surprisingly, they trade at fairly low P/E multiples. Low P/E stocks are assumed to have either greater risk than the average market or lower growth prospects. The low P/Es of the homebuilders are telling us that the housing market is indeed risky and that the stock market investors don't expect the game to last much longer. If you honestly believe that home prices are going to continue to appreciate for five to ten years into the future by double-digit annual percentages, the smart move is not to buy a house, but to buy call options on the homebuilders. If you are right about home prices, the homebuilders' stocks are dramatically undervalued and you will make many times your investment as they continue to climb, reflecting their increased earnings in the future and the eventual recovery of their P/Es to a more normal market level.

Frustratingly, homebuilders' stock prices do tell us something about the overall housing market, but it is just the opposite of what we hear from uninformed sources. No, their recent price levels do not suggest that the housing market is on stable ground. Rather, the stock market is sending a loud and clear warning that housing price levels are unsustainable, and reasonable stock market investors know it.

Theory 8: Home Prices Are Higher Because Incomes Are Higher

There is no economic reason that house prices should increase because incomes improve. Just because people have more money doesn't mean that they have to spend it on their homes. Houses are just like other consumption goods. Their price depends on how inexpensively they can be built, not how rich the purchaser is. Personal computers went down in price even as people's incomes increased because productivity enhancements let producers make PCs less expensively. Similarly, one would expect homes to come down in price as we think of smarter ways to build them using more productive tools and less expensive materials.

This is seen most clearly in Figure 2.3, which is the one-hundred-year-long history of real home prices. Real prices of homes during the first ninety years did not increase at all, and yet incomes increased substantially over the period. Productivity enhancements meant that average real incomes of households increased more than fivefold over this time period. People ended up spending less of their incomes on housing and shelter expenses, just what you would expect in a progressively richer society. It is only with the dramatic increase in home prices in the last nine years that people have spent a greater percentage of their incomes on housing.

This is because over the last nine years home prices have far outstripped household income growth. Since 1997 real home prices have increased some 65 percent while household incomes have increased less than 20 percent. Some analysts like to compare house prices to incomes, but even by this measure home price growth recently has far outstripped income growth.

This is not to say that wealthy Americans may not choose to spend larger amounts of their income on their homes. People with money can choose to spend it however they like. But at these price levels, individuals who pay high prices for homes should realize that the monies they are spending are pure personal consumption dollars and do not involve investing. Homebuyers who choose to pay millions of dollars for their homes and live in them have to realize that they are consuming whatever investment value there is in the home by occupying it, and at these prices there is very little chance they will be able to recoup their purchase price in the future. If they insist on calling it an investment, at best it can be considered a bad investment.

There is no economic reason that houses should increase in price as incomes increase. Historically, they have done just the opposite, except for the last nine years where artificial home price increases have far outstripped even income growth.

There is nothing inherently productive about putting money into an expensive home. In essence, it is money that is withheld from the markets where it might cause an increase in productivity. It is dead capital that might as well be put in a mattress, given how poor it helps future economic growth. We shall see in chapter 9 what might motivate a homebuyer to spend inordinate amounts of money relative to his income on his home and himself.

There are two additional and important theories as to why home prices are deservedly high. In chapter 6, I will debunk a theory popular among economists: that home prices are high because restrictive government regulations prevent new homes from being built to relieve the demand for housing. In chapter 7, I'll look in some detail at the most popular argument, that home prices go up when interest rates go down, and ask if that is "the" explanation of high home prices.

6

Is Government Regulation Preventing New Home Construction?

Surprisingly, the most frequent explanation economists and academics give for high current home prices is one that many people are not even familiar with. Many academics believe that the reason that home prices are high is that the government is improperly restricting the supply of new homes by limiting construction in many of our towns and cities across America. They got this idea from a very influential series of academic papers written over the last five years by Edward Glaeser of Harvard University and Joseph Gyourko of the Wharton School at the University of Pennsylvania.

But is this theory right?

The concept Glaeser and Gyourko introduced is that housing prices cannot increase in a city or neighborhood unless the new supply of housing is constrained somehow, as through governmental zoning restrictions or other local governmental building restrictions. Their logic is that the price of housing is composed of three distinct elements: the underlying cost of construction of the building itself, the acquisition cost of the land the home is constructed on, and the value associated with the legal right one has gained to be able to build on the property. In essence, you can have a physical house and a piece of property, but unless you have the land properly zoned for residential construction and have the necessary governmental building permits, you can't build a home. Just as the building and the land have value to you, so too does this right to build also have real value.

Glaeser and Gyourko demonstrated that the construction cost of the physical building we call a house by itself was less than the market cost of a home in almost every city in America. In some areas, in the big cities on the coasts, for example, the prices at which homes sold were many multiples of the replacement cost of the construction involved. (Chapter 5 contains a more thorough description of these findings on construction costs.)

If homes were selling for big premiums to the necessary costs of building them, then homebuilders should be profit-motivated to build more homes. We have all seen homes that sell for millions of dollars that couldn't cost more than $300,000 if built from scratch. Why is it that developers don't build more homes in these pricey areas and close the supposed value gap between new construction costs and the market values of homes?

The value of Glaeser and Gyourko's research is that it offers a rational explanation of why not all areas of the United States are participating equally in the housing price boom. In those areas of the Midwest, Southeast, and the Mountain West where land is relatively inexpensive and there are few restrictions on new building, nothing prevents builders from erecting new homes when prices tick upward. It is this new supply of homes, the authors argue, that moderates housing prices in these areas and prevents excessive real estate escalation. It is the form of arbitrage we refered to earlier in chapter 5 in which builders see an opportunity to profit from the shortage of homes and quickly turn inexpensive wood and nails into salable and valuable homes.

This research is important if only for this finding. It makes no sense to speculate in real estate prices in Utah or the flatlands of Texas where any increased prices due to increased demand will be met by unconstrained new building on inexpensive land, which is sure to moderate price increases and keep them in line with construction costs. If you are going to speculate in residential real estate, this study suggests you focus your efforts in areas in which raw land is scarce, new development is frowned upon, and zoning and building restrictions make new construction difficult.

In an innovative test in a 2003 article in the *Economic Policy Review* entitled "The Impact of Zoning on Housing Affordability," Glaeser and Gyourko ask a fundamental question. What is the acreage under your house worth, compared to what the extra acreage attached to your home is valued at in the market? They believe that if it is land scarcity that is driving the extra value seen in housing sales, this question will yield similar results for both pieces of property. In essence, land is land, and it should be valued the same regardless of whether a home is built on it or it sits adjacent to a home. But if government zoning laws and building regulations are preventing you from building on the "extra" land, then one would expect to find a steep premium in price between the land under your house, which by definition is zoned for housing and the extra attached land that is probably not zoned for development.

Although their statistical results are quite weak from an empirical standpoint, they report a rather startling conclusion. They find that the land under your house is worth as much as ten times the value of the land that might sit adjacent to your house. This finding clearly violates their assumption that if the value difference is due solely to the price of land, the two parcels should be found to be nearly equal in value. They then conclude that it must be zoning restrictions that are driving this price difference in land and place the blame for the lack of new home construction solely on government regulation rather than a malfunctioning of the free market for homes.

I believe the authors made a fundamental error in their analysis at this point. If the authors had been looking at homes built on quarter-acre plots and compared them to similar homes with ten acres of attached land it would be hard not to conclude that some sort of restriction must be in place that prevented the development of the raw land. If this were the case, it would be economically surprising if the quarter acre under the house was valued at $10 million per acre while the ten acres of undeveloped land next door were only valued at $1 million per acre. Surely the economically rational man would see the opportunity in such a tight housing environment to break up the ten acres into forty quarter-acre residential plots and sell them for $100 million in total, netting himself a $90 million profit. That is, unless as the authors suggest, he was prevented from doing so by an overly restrictive government.

But the data that these authors used did not involve single homes with tens of excess acres attached. Rather, they performed a statistical analysis of the homes in various cities in America that on average have much less "extra" land attached to them. The home lot sizes they analyzed differed by city, but, in general, they were not looking at tens of additional acres of raw land attached to the home, rather typically more like only an additional 3,000 to 5,000 square feet. (There are 43,560 square feet to one acre.)

At a little less than an eighth of an acre, 5,000 square feet is much less land than is typically required for a residential development project. As a matter of fact, it would be hard to fit one additional home on such a plot. After allowing for front and back yards, swimming pools, undevelopable hillsides and mountains, and naturally standing water in ponds and lakes, this probably is not enough extra land to build a single new house, regardless of what the zoning laws say. If this is the case, then it makes perfect sense that it would be worth considerably less than a plot of land sufficient for building a home. Land suitable for a home is always more valuable than rough small plots unsuitable for building because humans put so much value on their homes. There would not be any housing shortage if people were as comfortable in tents by the side of the road as they are in their own cozy homes.

The authors set out to explain why houses were not more affordable to the nation's more modest income citizens and uncovered a rather confusing explanation and suggested solution. Under their analysis, the reason that there was not more modestly priced housing available was that local governments were restricting the building of new houses. Their solution was to recommend the dismantling of many local zoning ordinances that prevented new residential construction, which should ease housing prices in the future.

But, in reality, what the authors had uncovered was that these supposed "restricted" areas were predominately in the wealthiest towns and neighborhoods of our country. And if my critique of their work is correct, the "excess" supply of raw land they had uncovered was in such small plots on average as to be effectively undevelopable.

What the authors really uncovered in their analysis was that wealthier neighborhoods typically have larger attached properties than poor neighborhoods. The authors were, in effect, saying that the housing shortage and affordability problem could be solved if we only allowed the building of a low-income house on the front lawn of every big house in Beverly Hills.

This of course was not their conclusion. They stated very strongly that they had discovered the real reason for the recent run-up in prices and the villain was the same as always—big bad government and burdensome regulation. This message was picked up by other free market academics and media pundits and, because of the reputation of the authors and apparent thoroughness of their work, quickly broadcast as the "true" reason why home prices had escalated to such heights recently.

It was a convenient explanation. People like to have a villain and recently they have gotten very comfortable blaming government for their problems. For the free market crowd it was perfect; a market anomaly like bubble real estate prices could be explained by the inexcusable interference of the government in the marketplace. Unfortunately, for them, the analysis was not right.

It is true that it is easier to attain housing price increases in regions of the country that have a scarcity of land and some degree of zoning restrictions on future building. One might even argue that it is a necessary condition before home prices can rise faster than underlying construction costs. But the basic premise of the Glaeser and Gyourko papers was wrong. It was not the zoning restrictions that had driven up the price of the homes in these exclusive communities. Rather it was the underlying value of the raw land that had been pushed higher by scarcity concerns as well as exclusivity issues we will address further in chapter 9.

So going back to the authors' original question, how does the value of a home divide between its construction costs, its land value, and its legal rights to development? The tide has now turned. There is no proof that it is restricted development that is causing the price differential, so it is much more likely that the explanation is that it is raw land that is either scarce or overpriced in these highly-priced communities. And this is what we see when we examine these exclusive communities in detail. Not only do most of these exclusive communities with the biggest housing price increases of late not have any available raw land left to develop, many of them are building extra houses on every square foot that will support it. Many new homes are being constructed and squeezed between two older homes in these exclusive enclaves. Most of the developable land in these high-priced areas has already been developed.

Homeowners in our wealthiest and most overpriced cities should not take great comfort in finding that it is the raw land value that is driving up their home values. While it may appear that land values are more substantial and less ephemeral than values created through restricted zoning, this may be an illusion. San Diego has seen a dramatic increase in its home prices over the last nine years. It appears that the increase is mainly due to an increase in land values as people have come to appreciate the wonderful climate and excellent outdoor activities available there. But just because San Diego has a limited coastline or has run out of development land near the coast where one can build single-family homes does not assure that recent housing price increases will stick permanently.

San Diego has begun doing what any major city does when it runs out of real estate. It has started building up, and with great success. Its new condominium high-rise apartments downtown sell for up to $1 to $2 million each, not a large discount to the area's better single-family homes. While single-family homes are typically larger, with private yards and pools, some of these condos come with views of the city and the ocean to die for. With tennis courts, concierges, car services, and workout gyms, they provide an interesting alternative to living in single-family homes. As such, you would expect the price appreciation of single-family homes in San Diego to be moderated somewhat by the growth of new condos heading up to the sky, but to date we have witnessed no slowing in the growth of home prices in San Diego.

In addition to containing an error in their analysis, the authors' conclusions do not explain the evidence presented earlier in chapter 3. If zoning restrictions in America were the key to explaining the recent run-up in prices, why have prices increased globally? And if these restrictive cities have had long histories of regulation and zoning restrictions, why is it only in the last twenty-five years that real housing prices have taken off? If these towns are so restrictive to new building, why haven't their rents also increased? If there is a housing shortage because of a restriction on new building, it should impact both the owner and renter market equally. Finally, if zoning restrictions explain it all, why are the homebuilders showing such large profits? Don't they face the same zoning restrictions?

The argument that restricting new housing growth somehow can cause housing price increases is fundamentally flawed. The increased supply of homes on the market through new construction is a small percentage of the total number of houses sold. The supply of homes available for sale in a market can increase without any change in the supply of new homes. As prices increase in a market, it is natural that some existing homeowners will find the higher prices attractive and agree to put their homes on the market. Some may take their profits and leave for less expensive areas, some may agree to rent rather than repurchase another home, but as prices go up, one would expect the supply of existing homes offered for sale should increase.

Glaeser and Gyourko recognize that solely restricting supply does not cause local prices to increase automatically unless there is also increased demand, but this point has been lost on many of the pundits who mistakenly cite their work. A manufacturing city in the Midwest that is losing jobs globally and suffering a decline in overall population can enact dozens of restrictive and exclusive zoning and building policies and they still will not experience any substantial housing price appreciation. As Glaeser and Gyourko realized, to experience unusual housing price increases you must also have an unusual demand for housing. They were not able to identify what might be driving this unusual demand, but I try to address it in chapters 7, 8, and 9.

In a subsequent article in the *Journal of Law and Economics* entitled "Why Is Manhattan So Expensive?" Glaeser, Gyourko, and Saks move from middle America to its biggest city, New York, to try to further strengthen their claims that it is zoning and building restrictions that are the culprit in higher home prices. They chose Manhattan because, in their opinion, population density is so high there already that there can be no social cost to building two or three additional stories on any *new* skyscrapers. By adding to the planned height of *new* Manhattan skyscrapers they avoid the land valuation problem since the same plot of land can support building either the original design or one slightly taller. They view the only additional cost as the marginal construction cost of adding three new floors to the top of the building. Because builders are not building ever-taller high-rises, and because it appears to be extremely profitable relative to the forecasted construction costs, the authors once again conclude that the reason people are not doing it must be because of overly restrictive building regulations.

When one thinks of Manhattan, one thinks of buildings so tall that if they were indeed two or three stories taller it really wouldn't make much difference in terms of congestion or overcrowding. But the authors help us by picking a particular neighborhood to make their point. Carnegie Hill is an old, historically German neighborhood near 90th Street and Third Avenue and home to Woody Allen and Alan Alda and the famous writers' restaurant, Elaine's. But a visit to Carnegie Hill shows at once what is wrong with the authors' assumptions. Carnegie Hill is a lovely neighborhood, composed of mostly low-rise apartment buildings and condos with friendly neighborhood delicatessens and movie theaters and beautiful views of not just other buildings but the wide open skies of New York.

Clearly, adding one very large high-rise to this area would ruin the view many of the residents have from their apartments. More importantly, adding lots of high-rise apartments to Carnegie Hill would ruin the neighborhood. The sidewalks would become congested, it would be impossible to find cabs, traffic would stall, subways would become overcrowded, and the neighborhood's charm would vanish.

The authors fail to recognize this enormous cost to the local residents. In some sort of attempt at social utopia, they suggest that the greater good could be achieved for the greatest number by violating the rights of the existing residents to determine the structure of their own neighborhood and instead force upon them increased new housing development. Just because the new high-rises would sell out does not mean anyone would be better off. Certainly, the residents of the old neighborhood would be worse off. And if this type of logic were extended to every city in America, all communities and homeowners would be worse off. Part of the appeal of property ownership and involvement in a community is the right to decide how much growth and development is permissible. Under the authors' plan, the greater good can be achieved by violating local neighborhoods' rights to determine the amount of development they will allow. To suggest that the cause of the high prices of condos in New York is due to Woody Allen and the other residents of Carnegie Hill preventing high-rise construction in their neighborhood really misses the point entirely. Under this logic, neighborhoods would have to support unlimited new-building construction and congestion until home prices had a real reason to decline—the neighborhood would have been ruined.

Zoning restrictions are not always bad. Government regulation is not always bad. Sometimes, local government regulation is exactly what the residents want. Surprise: the local government is the people. In a properly working local government, new regulations reflect the desires of the people living in the neighborhood. If Greenwich, Connecticut, wants to maintain some sense of exclusivity and natural beauty by restricting home building to lots at least two acres in size, who is to say that this policy is wrong? Doesn't each neighborhood have control over its own destiny? If the acreage requirement is shrunk to one acre, it is not obvious that the total value of all Greenwich acreage would increase or decrease. Maybe the land is worth more and is better utilized economically in two-acre lots. Even if the total value of all land in Greenwich were worth less as two-acre lots, this would not be justification for overruling what the local residents wishes are with regard to development of their neighborhoods. Glaeser, Gyourko et. al can talk about the social cost of not allowing full development of larger, more densely spaced buildings, but they need also to discuss the social cost of violating individual's property rights and the rights of a local community to decide how it wishes to develop on its own. Once these individual and collective rights are violated, slight potential increases in land utilization benefits may seem awfully small in comparison.

Rather than concluding that zoning and government regulation are the problem, a different interpretation could lead to just the opposite conclusion. If you look at the location of the highest priced homes in America, you'll find them mostly in cities in the blue states, namely, those states that have supported Democratic presidential candidates recently. Seattle, Portland, Boston, New York, Miami, Los Angeles, San Francisco, Sacramento—these are not only the cities with the highest home prices and the greatest recent housing price appreciation, these are also traditionally Democratic Party strongholds. Why would these liberal bastions also have the highest and fastest-growing house prices?

Surprisingly to some, cities that have the highest degree of local government and citizen involvement have become our most desirable and our most livable. Houses are five times more expensive in San Francisco than in Buffalo because more people want to live by the bay. Heck, even Milton Friedman lives in San Francisco. He may criticize government involvement in the markets in his writings, but when he goes to bed at night he sleeps in the capital of social activism and good local government. The authors of this research paper never suggest it, but their own data confirm that the best-governed, best-regulated cities in America have created a living environment that homeowners will pay a premium for in higher home prices.

Glaeser and Gyourko's work is often cited by individuals trying to claim that the majority of the country could not be at risk of a housing crash since much of the country has responded to increased demand for housing by building more. It is true that housing in these middle states may not appreciate as rapidly, due to the continued increases in the supply of new homes, but this does not mean they are immune from a price decline in housing in the future.

Builders in mid-American states where land and development are plentiful are constantly building to keep up with increased demand for homes. But what if that demand was not a stable long-term demand but rather reflected more ephemeral conditions such as overly aggressive mortgage lending? When that artificial demand exits the overpriced coasts, it is clear that housing prices will drop closer to replacement cost. What will happen if that same artificially created demand is reduced in the middle of the country or if the national economy weakens and reduces housing demand there?

The answer of course is that the middle of the country is also at risk of housing price declines. The reason is that these states may have overbuilt in reaction to a short-term, somewhat phony stimulus to demand. Once banks pull back and stop their aggressive lending, these states in Middle America may find that they have built more housing than they actually need and at higher price points than is appropriate. Prices could very well fall in these states, possibly even below the level of replacement construction costs. If a declining manufacturing center in the Midwest is overbuilt because of the aggressiveness of bank lending, then when that lending stops there is no reason why prices should not decline to a level reflective of the job outlook for the area. There is no rule that new homes have to be worth what it cost to build them. If phony demand created by easy credit drove the construction in the first place, then it would be logical to assume that once that demand evaporates, prices might settle below the cost of construction.

This is an important concept because it shows that the entire country is at risk of a possible housing price correction, even those areas in the middle of the country that have not experienced rapid growth in prices lately. While their overbuilding was successful in moderating price increases, it may be the very cause of a nationwide housing decline once the artificially induced demand is removed.

The dramatic cost difference between homes is not in zoning restrictions but in raw land costs. An acre of land in the Midwest can cost $20,000, in Los Angeles $13 million, and in Manhattan $70 million. Land is becoming more scarce in our most exclusive communities, but that still does not answer the question why people would pay such a large premium to live in these communities. I'll answer that question in chapter 9, and look more closely at the scope of possible price declines in chapter 11.

7

The Real Culprit—
Overly Aggressive Banks

In order for home prices to reach irrational levels, numerous willing parties need to play a role. We have seen in chapter 6 that a real scarcity of land or severe restrictions on new development can be causes of house prices growing much faster than construction costs.

But this is not enough. Scarce land and restrictions on growth do not automatically imply overvalued house prices. Cities in Alaska that are land-constrained by natural configurations like rivers and mountain ranges still have reasonably priced homes.

No, there are other fundamental forces in addition to supply constraints that must be in place before home prices can escalate. First, because few people can afford to purchase such an expensive asset as a house outright for cash, there must be a willing source of financing. The lender not only has to be generous in the amounts he will lend, but has to be willing to extend money to a buyer who may be overpaying. This is not easy because most rational lenders will realize that price declines in the future will result in the evaporation of a home's equity and turn a relatively secure financing into one that looks suspiciously like a zero-equity loan. Typically, lenders like to have a real equity cushion below them so that any future price declines do not immediately cause the value of their loan's collateral to decline below the mortgage amount.

Next, and very importantly, there must be a desire by the purchaser to buy the home at an inflated price. We say "desire" rather than "demand" because we want to give some indication that this type of overpaying behavior may go far beyond normal economic demand and enter the realm of psychological need. If homes are overvalued, and the buyer knows it, there is no conventional economic explanation for why he or she would complete the purchase. Either the buyers are unaware of the high prices being paid; they are indifferent as they realize they are playing with other people's money; there is an option component to their returns; or they are getting some psychic reward that economists are less likely to recognize and measure. We will return to this question of noneconomic returns to the homeowner in chapter 9.

There is a final element that must be in place before astronomically high prices can be paid and justified as true and stable indicators of long-term housing value. The buyer must be able to afford the home and choose to buy instead of settling on other economic alternatives. Again, housing purchases are such large acquisitions for the typical family that the amount they can pay is very dependent on their projected incomes, which are highly dependent on the state of the economy in the future. You may want to live in a 7,000-square-foot mansion in Beverly Hills, but if you don't have sufficient income you can forget it. Similarly, when the entire economy of a region crashes, one would expect more people to lose their jobs and have difficulty with their mortgage payments. Housing prices should reflect a region's average income levels for this reason.

Of course, the homebuyer always has alternatives that must be examined in determining the appropriateness of house prices. Because he could always rent rather than buy, it is only logical that there should be a fairly stable relationship between purchase prices and rents. Because people can always move to a new city, housing prices should reflect the amenities and advantages available in one city as compared to another. Because he can always sell, prices should never get so high that the homeowner can withdraw his funds from real estate and place them in alternative investments for a substantially greater return.

So, there seem to be five necessary conditions before housing prices can increase substantially. First, the supply of new homes must be constrained, either through high land prices or restrictive zoning. Second, substantial financing must be available to support the planned acquisition price. Third, buyers must have the desire to own the property at the high price. Fourth, the buyer must have sufficient income to afford the price paid. And lastly, there must not be a better alternative way, such as renting and investing, for the prospective owner to accomplish the same objective.

In chapter 6, I discussed the constraint on the supply of new homes and the fact that exclusive communities with a scarcity of land are going to be the likely area for the greatest potential home-price appreciation. In chapter 9, I will talk more about the mysterious allure of home ownership and what drives seemingly rational human beings to pay astronomical prices for their homes. In this chapter, I will concentrate on what I believe to be the prime reason we are seeing real estate prices escalating in many countries and cities around the world—namely, easily available financing from the banks. Regardless of how crazy an individual homebuyer might be, or how badly he or she wants to overspend on the purchase of a home, none of this would be possible without very willing and aggressive mortgage lenders. To understand the story from the lender's perspective I need to digress and review how interest rates affect home values.

The reason most people give for the recent boom in housing prices is that interest rates are low. Everybody knows that when rates decline, more people can borrow more money, and housing values increase. In fact, this isn't necessarily true.

Conventional wisdom compares the housing market to the stock market. When interest rates decline, stock values and price-to-earnings ratios increase. Again, unfortunately, this is not necessarily true.

As a matter of fact, typically when nominal interest rates decline a substantial amount, there is absolutely no positive change in the true inherent value of homes or common stocks.

To see why, remember the difference between nominal interest rates and real interest rates. Nominal interest rates are the rates published and discussed in the newspaper. To find the real rate of interest, subtract the expected rate of inflation from this nominal or stated rate. For example, if stated or nominal interest rates are 15 percent, and inflation is expected to be 12 percent per year, then the real interest rate is 3 percent.

It is important to subtract general inflation rates to determine real interest rates because general inflation affects all prices and therefore has no real direct long-term economic impact. General inflation is typically caused by the government printing money to fund budget deficits. Because there is more currency chasing the same amount of goods, all goods have to increase in price, measured in the inflated currency that is in circulation. Prices go up 12 percent, wages go up 12 percent, houses go up 12 percent, the money supply increases by 12 percent, interest rates are 15 percent rather than 3 percent, a difference of 12 percent—but nothing has really changed in the economy. The same amount of goods are produced and consumed, and you should be able to afford to live in the same house.

So when interest rates make a big move downward, say from 15 to 6 percent, it is typically expected inflation that is changing, and the real rate is not affected. In this example, inflation could have declined from 12 to 3 percent, driving nominal interest rates from 15 to 6 percent, but leaving real interest rates unchanged at 3 percent.

And if real interest rates don't change, there shouldn't be any real impact on prices. What we have experienced worldwide is a twenty-year period of lower nominal interest rates due to inflation getting burned out of the world economy, but there is no evidence that the real rate of interest has changed materially, if at all.

Nominal interest rates have declined dramatically in many countries of the world over the last twenty years, but real interest rates have stayed relatively constant, near their historical level of approximately 3 percent. If this is the case, then housing prices shouldn't have increased at all due to the nominal rate decline. For the first time in recorded history many of the advanced countries of the world have lived through a period of dramatic disinflation.

To see this more clearly, let us return to the concept of housing P/Es discussed in chapter 3. Remember, a housing P/E is constructed by dividing the price of a home by the rental income it could attain in the marketplace. As we saw, this housing P/E multiple has expanded by some 47 percent over the last five years, growing from 11 to more than 17 times on average for the entire country's housing stock.

People naturally assumed that this expansion of the average housing multiple was the result of declining interest rates. But if we are right, and the reason rates declined was inflation burning out of the economy, then real rates did not change during the period.

If real interest rates didn't change, then real housing P/E multiples should not have changed.

A house's P/E is composed of its price divided by its rental income stream. If inflation is 10 percent, then the house's nominal price might be 10 percent higher in a year, but so would its rental income. The numerator and the denominator would both be 10 percent higher in a world of 10 percent inflation, so the P/E of the house would not change. Similarly, any assumed change in general inflation, either up or down, will impact both the price and the rental stream equally over time and will completely cancel each other out. If nominal interest rates are declining because inflation is easing, there is no reason why real rates should change. Real housing prices and housing P/Es should be constant.

So something very strange is happening here. Real housing prices are rising in nearly every single country of the world that is experiencing a decline in nominal interest rates and yet theory tells us that a change in nominal rates, with no change in underlying real rates, should not affect house prices. Is there a secondary effect that solves this conundrum?

To see what actually is happening, let's look at the problem from the perspective of the financing institution that funds home purchases, namely, the commercial banks. The primary tool commercial banks utilize in their determination of how much money to lend to a prospective home purchaser is the bank's qualifying formula. It has gotten more complicated with the advent of computers, but at its most basic it is still a first-year test of how comfortable the prospective buyer is in making his required mortgage payments given his current salary or income.

While a borrower is not required to spend all the money he or she qualifies for, in the competitive world of house prices that is often exactly what ends up happening. Most of the formulas the banks utilize are some sort of ratio of your income in the first year to your total annual mortgage payments in the first year. And this is the problem. Mortgages are complex, sometimes thirty- to forty-year instruments. No adequate credit analysis can be reduced to a simple formula that focuses solely on the first year's coverage of mortgage interest, especially in a world of variable inflation rates. So, when a bank officer talks about the percentage of pretax income that should go to a mortgage payment, or when she says you can afford a house equal to seven or eight times your current household income, please realize that this is a very simplistic analysis. Such an analysis can lead to very different results in differing interest rate and inflation environments.

These simple first-year-ratio bank-qualifying formulas may be behind the entire worldwide bubble in residential real estate prices. Imagine that—the entire world's real estate may be overvalued because bankers are all using similar shorthand analyses to determine appropriate lending amounts, and those analyses may have fatal flaws. To visualize these flaws we need a real-world example. Let's look at real estate prices in the United States today compared to and what they were twenty-five years ago, when inflation was much worse. Here we will focus on the inflation-adjusted prices of real estate so a one dollar increase in price represents a real return of one dollar.

In 1980, general inflation was 12 percent and nominal interest rates were at 15 percent, so real interest rates were 3 percent. In real terms, nothing much has changed today. Inflation, for these purposes, can be assumed to have declined today to 2 percent per year, interest rates are 5 percent, so the real rate of interest is still 3 percent. Because real rates haven't changed, and because real cash rent flows from the house haven't changed, the house should not have changed in value, in real terms, or in constant dollars. Let us examine what the banks would have lent us then and today, in real terms, to see if we can understand why there is so much money chasing housing today.

If your household income was $60,000 (in real 2005 constant dollars), you could have qualified for a loan and bought a home in 1985 for $143,000 (real 2005 dollars), assuming you put 10 percent down and satisfied the bank's requirement that no more than one-third of your income went to your first year's mortgage payment. And this is the key. Not only was the loan amount and the suggested price paid conservative on day one, but the loan would look better and better over time. Five years later, your salary would have been expected to grow to $105,000 due to general price inflation alone (assuming no real increase in your salary, just keeping up with monetary growth and general inflation). In that fifth year your mortgage would have been very secure, as only 17 percent of your future salary would have been needed to cover your fifth-year mortgage payment. In this example, your salary is growing at the general inflation rate, but your monthly mortgage cost is fixed and stable, thus you look like a much better credit risk each year, due to general inflation alone.

Contrast that with today's world of lower nominal interest rates. Using the same bank qualifying formula, that one-third of your first year's salary should go to your mortgage payments, the bank now says you qualify for a $440,000 house. Your coverage of interest payments in the first year is the same as in the high inflation example above. But not for long. In the fifth year out, your household income only increases at the expected 2 percent inflation rate each year, so your income in the fifth year is only $66,000. In the fifth year, it takes 27 percent of your income to cover the expected mortgage payment, not the 17 percent in the high-inflation example above.

And the example only worsens if you make further assumptions based on today's bank market for mortgage loans. If you assume your loan has a floating rate, interest only is due each year, and a bank allows you a 40 percent mortgage-to-income ratio, the bank will qualify you for the purchase of a $660,000 house and it will take 36 percent of your expected income in the fifth year to make your mortgage payment. If you assume your loan is floating-rate and rates increase 3 percent over the next five years, it will take an astounding 66 percent of your household income to make the mortgage payment in the fifth year.

Reality, of course, can be even worse than these numbers indicate. The reason is that this example assumes that your household income remains constant in real terms. But we know that the people who have trouble with their mortgages are those that have had a very real decline in their disposable income, usually due to an unforeseen sickness or death of a loved one, a divorce, or job loss.

Homebuyers who have taken out adjustable-rate mortgages must have done a similar calculation on the back of an envelope when they signed up for the loan. Somehow, they gained confidence in knowing they could always sell the house if disaster struck, or if interest rates increased before the time came when their first mortgage interest would be reset. But if the majority of the buyers are utilizing the same type of thinking, and everybody tries to sell when rates tick up and their mortgages reprice, the market price for housing may drop precipitously. The option of selling into a healthy housing market evaporates at exactly the time you really need it, when rates have increased and ARM borrowers are facing higher mortgage payments than they can afford. Panic selling will drive prices down further, as few will be able to face the dramatically increased mortgage payments required as rates rise.

So, here we have examined two different interest rate environments, one with high inflation and one without. Surprisingly, the banks' lending formulas have somehow led to much greater home values in the low inflation environment, even though in real terms nothing has changed. Real cash flows, that is, real rents, have not changed, and real interest rates have not changed, and yet now a home that sold for a real price of $143,000 sells easily in today's marketplace for $660,000. The loans look very similar from a qualifying formula perspective, but there is one very important difference. In the 1985 example, you were paying about 2.4 times your salary for your home, today you are paying 11 times your salary for your home. The house is exactly the same, the first year's coverage of your mortgage interest payment is very similar, but you just paid $517,000 more for the same house. You may not feel it on day one, but the primary difference is this: you have an additional mortgage amount of $465,000 with your name on it.

And general inflation cannot be counted on to inflate your salary and get you out of this mess. You are going to have this debt around your neck for years to come. If things go well, every waking hour will go to its repayment. If things go poorly, the housing market will decline and you will be left paying off a mortgage on a property whose value is less than the mortgage amount. Or, if worse came to worse, a medical emergency or job loss could lead you to miss mortgage payments in the future and you could lose the house to foreclosure. And not only will you lose the house, but in most states you will remain liable for any deficiency between the forced auction price the bank realizes on its sale and your mortgage loan balance. You could easily lose your family's home and still have hundreds of thousands of dollars of debt facing you, often when your cash flows are impaired due to sickness or job loss.

So here is one example of how a very simple formula that bankers utilize to help them determine lending amounts may be what is causing the entire worldwide appreciation in real estate prices. And this price appreciation isn't real. It is not due to lower real interest rates or greater expected real rental incomes in the future. It is solely due to banks' overall aggressiveness in their lending formulas during a period of declining worldwide inflation.

We mentioned earlier in this chapter that it is conventional wisdom that stock market prices and common stock P/Es also rise when interest rates decline. But if the decline in interest rates is solely nominal, that is, there is no change in real interest rates, then the stock market has the same valuation problem we have described here for housing. Namely, how can stock prices and stock P/Es rise if there is no change in real interest rates?

This puzzle was first discussed in a famous academic paper written in 1979 by Franco Modigliani and R. A. Cohn. Modigliani and Cohn realized that the stock market's P/E multiple indeed did seem to be expanding as nominal rates declined, but realizing that the underlying real interest rate was unchanged led them to ask how and why? Their explanation is one of the first papers that claimed a major pricing inefficiency in the stock market. In effect, the authors claim that buyers in the stock market mistakenly discounted real cash flows at high nominal interest rates rather than real interest rates. If correct, this meant that investors were dramatically undervaluing stocks during periods of high inflation. Their work is still much discussed today as it is a prime example of the teachings of the behavioral economics school that markets are not always correct in their pricing and that market participants do not always act rationally and correctly in valuing investments. If correct, such a conclusion would drive a dagger through efficient free marketers' claims that markets are a good way of determining prices, that participants act rationally, and that the prices that result are fair and unbiased.

I personally do not believe the Modigliani explanation of why stock prices tend to track nominal rather than real interest rates. If it is not true, then an alternative explanation must be found that explains why the market goes down when inflation is high. Rather than looking for an anomaly in the stock market itself, is there something out in the real economy that would cause real economic activity to decline during periods of high inflation? If so, maybe this real decline in expected earnings is what is driving low stock market valuations during periods of high inflation and not the misapplication of high nominal interest rates in discounting future cash flows. But how could general inflation, that is supposed to affect all prices and wages equally, have a negative impact on the stock market?

Maybe we have already uncovered the cause. Perhaps it is the mortgage banking industry itself and its qualifying formulas that are the actual culprits. I have conjectured previously in this chapter that banks may be underlending to the housing sector during periods of high inflation because their qualifying formulas do not take adequate account of higher salaries in the future due to inflation. If during periods of high inflation the banks lend less money to homebuyers, this would cause a general retraction in the housing, homebuilding, renovation, furniture, and mortgage sectors. A pullback in lending to some of the world's biggest industries might cause an economic decline that could easily spread to the entire economy as jobs are lost and consumption declines. A similar real economic decline would hit in other big asset industries like automobiles during high inflation periods as car buyers are also overly restricted in the amount of lending they qualify for.

So, according to this explanation, a very real economic recession occurs and forecasted earnings of companies decline solely due to a bout of high general price inflation. The stock market would properly discount the future earnings of its companies, not because of investor error in selecting a nominal interest rate, but because real growth of earnings in the economy will be stalling. And this is what we see in the historical analysis. The stock market moves counter-cyclically with inflation. When inflation is high, stocks head lower. This makes no sense because stocks represent real companies with real earnings that should keep up with inflation. If investors are indeed rational and markets do indeed work, then the only explanation is that inflation is causing real growth in earnings and cash flow to slow. And if we are right, in high-inflation eras the commercial banks and their darned qualifying formulas are the culprits actually slowing economic growth. By underlending to housing during high-inflation periods, the commercial banks starve the housing sector for needed funds and plant the seeds of a future recession.

To summarize, we have discovered that most of the advanced countries of the world that have realized an easing of inflation over the last ten years and a decline in nominal, but not necessarily real interest rates, have experienced a striking increase of some 50 to 200 percent in home prices. If real interest rates have remained unchanged and the only change has been nominal or stated levels of rates, this is a real conundrum.

Similarly, the stock markets of the world seem to move inversely with inflation, that is, periods of high general inflation result in a collapse of market P/E multiples. Again, this makes little sense, as real interest rates rarely change dramatically as inflation increases.

The answer to both conundrums is one and the same: The qualifying formula banks use to determine the amount of money they will lend to eventual home purchasers has an implied error in it. Qualifying formulas are heavily weighted toward first-year ratios that take almost no account of future income growth due to general inflation. Therefore, banks underlend to homebuyers during periods of high inflation and overlend during periods of low inflation. This explains an explosion in housing prices worldwide over the last ten years as inflation has eased, nominal rates have declined, and lending has mushroomed. Surprisingly, it may also explain a twenty-five-year-old problem in financial economics, namely, why the stock market seems to move inversely to inflation and seems to undervalue real future earnings during periods of high inflation. The answer: During periods of high inflation the banks, as suggested by their own qualifying formulas, cut back financing to the housing and auto sectors and create the beginnings of a recessionary environment of lower real corporate earnings, which are then properly discounted by the stock market's always rational investors.

It may not seem like a big difference to the casual reader whether the bankers of the world or the stock investors of the world are making the error that drives these problems in both the housing market and the stock market. But to economists, there is a very fundamental difference. Sophisticated markets should be efficient and price their wares properly because there is always the opportunity for arbitragers to intercede and profit if financial assets are mispriced. There is no similar guarantee that private real asset markets like the housing market will work properly. You may now believe that the world's bankers are mispricing and misallocating mortgage money during periods of variable inflation, but there is no clear arbitrage opportunity available. You can start your own bank and try to do things correctly, but if you are going to be tight with money during periods of loose credit you probably won't have many customers. No, the only way you can profit from this knowledge is to be alert that housing prices are artificially elevated and will eventually return to earth. And be careful not to hold in your portfolio too many bank stocks that are heavily invested in residential real estate mortgages.

You may believe that indeed, this time, real rates have changed and that they are driving higher home prices. We have all heard explanations why this might be true. Globalization has increased productivity. China's excess funds invested in Treasuries prop up the United

States and keep real rates here low. There is a global savings glut. I am not moved by any of these explanations. Refer once again to Shiller's graph of real home prices over the last hundred years in Figure 2.3. It seems to suggest that, other than during the last ten years, real prices haven't changed materially over time. So if real rates have indeed declined lately, it is probably the first time in at least a hundred years that they have had a meaningful impact on housing prices.

An examination of the yield on securities called TIPS also suggests little change in the real interest rate. Treasury Inflation Protected Securities (TIPS) are bonds issued by the U.S. government with a promise to pay the holder a market-determined real rate of return plus whatever the rate of inflation turns out to be over the holding period. While the bonds have a narrow market and are not broadly owned, the real rate has always traded in the 1.5 to 3 percent range since TIPS were introduced in the 1990s.

Even if you believe that real interest rates have declined from 3 to 2 percent, this does not justify a 50 percent increase in home prices. Remember, if real rates are lower, it most likely indicates that real growth prospects for the economy are lower. Specifically, rental incomes expected from purchased properties would also be expected to grow at a slower rate. If real growth in rental income streams also dropped from 3 to 2 percent, then one would not expect any increase in housing prices. Certainly there are countries like Spain and Ireland that have seen their real economic growth rates increase as they have developed economically, and some of that expected future growth should find its way into higher rental incomes and higher home prices. But should house prices have increased ten to twelve times in these countries? And remember, unlike common stocks, the supply of homes can always be increased through new construction, thus moderating any dramatic home price increases.

Of course, the aggressiveness of banks in the lending of mortgage money to the housing market is not limited solely to the misapplication of their borrower-qualifying formulas. A perusal of any local newspaper will uncover banks that are lending mortgage money on much more aggressive terms today than even ten years ago. If anything can be learned from our qualifying-formula story above, it is that banks should require a smaller percentage of one's salary go to mortgage payments during periods of low inflation solely because we now understand that your salary is not going to magically grow you out of debt. But banks today are doing just the opposite. In today's world of lower inflation, banks have chosen to increase the percentage a mortgage payment is to salary from 30 to 40 percent and there are rumors that it exceeds 50 percent in many cases.

In the last ten years we have witnessed banks requiring significantly lower down payments or equity investment money in order to purchase a house. While 20 percent down used to be standard, today we hear deals done with 10 percent down, with zero down, or even transactions in which the banks lend more than the value of the home so that they can extract fees and the buyer can extract cash on day one. There are deals being done today with many more subprime borrowers who would not have qualified to buy a home under the old rules. We have mentioned that the banks and the Fed have pushed many more people into pursuing floating-rate ARM deals rather than traditional fixed-rate mortgages. Given that rates are near a historic low, the only reason to pursue such a risky strategy is so the homeowner can stretch on his or her purchase price. Even owners planning to sell in a short time frame should not subject themselves to the risk of increasing ARM mortgage payments, especially in a world of uncertain housing prices.

Mortgage bankers are proud of the panoply of mortgage products they have introduced in the last ten years. Interest-only mortgages, negative amortization loans, multiple option loans have all gained tremendous acceptance in the market and now represent some 35 percent of newly issued nationally. The sole purpose of such plans that lower the initial mortgage payment is to allow cash-tight buyers to stretch on the price they can pay for a home. Buyers who qualify for $400,000 of lending under a conventional mortgage may qualify for $500,000 under a floating-rate deal or even $550,000 if they defer paying back principal or if they let the loan balance grow over time.

If we are right that the availability of easy money from bankers is a primary reason for the real estate housing boom, then we ought to be able to find a way to test this supposition. If bankers in misapplying overly generous qualifying formulas and aggressively offering zero-down, floating-rate, interest-only deals, are saturating the housing markets with money, then we ought to be able to measure their effect statistically. Because bank money is the predominant source of financing for a home purchase, we would expect to see higher home prices in areas in which bankers are more active and lend more aggressively. For these purposes, we have removed the homebuyer from the equation and assumed that he spends nearly every dollar that he qualifies for. Let us see if we can establish a relationship between the location of the most aggressive commercial bankers and where housing prices have increased the fastest.

We have seen in chapter 3 that house prices in the wealthiest communities and cities in America have appreciated the most over the last ten years. This is most evident in the analysis of housing P/E expansions by city. Is there a reason to suggest that overly aggressive bankers might be the cause of this phenomenon? Why would bankers tend to be more active in the mortgage markets of wealthy communities than other neighborhoods in general?

Most wealthy neighborhoods have always had homes priced far above the national average. As such, it is common sense that the majority of mortgages in these very wealthy towns exceed the mandatory maximum size loan that would make them eligible for selling the loan through to Fannie Mae or Freddie Mac. Currently, these institutions will not accept any mortgages greater than $355,000. Any mortgage that exceeds this amount is called a jumbo mortgage and cannot be purchased by these federally supported institutions.

Most people in these wealthy, exclusive communities finance their home purchases with jumbo mortgages that are structured and bought by the commercial banks. Because these jumbo mortgages will never qualify for Fannie or Freddie packaging and resale, there is no reason to maintain Fannie's or Freddie's credit requirements. The banks are free to structure these jumbos as aggressively as they want. They can float. They can pay or not pay principal. No down payment—no problem.

So the first thing we would expect to find is a much greater participation of commercial banks in these wealthy communities' mortgage activities due to the fact that jumbo mortgages represent such a larger percentage of total mortgage financing than in a less prosperous community. If our thesis is correct, then greater commercial bank involvement in these wealthy cities and communities will involve more aggressive and increased mortgage lending and lead to faster home price appreciation. A simple regression analysis across many cities performed by the author shows exactly that. With some 99.5 percent statistical confidence, the wealthiest communities five years ago in terms of levels of housing prices have experienced the highest home price appreciation since then. One plausible explanation of this data is that these cities have had a disproportionate level of involvement by the overly aggressive banks through jumbo mortgages and their cheaply available bank funds have been the driving force behind the recent home price appreciation. We saw in chapter 6 that it is the same wealthy communities that are most likely to have scarce raw land resources to dedicate to any new building. In chapter 9 I will explore a further reason why individuals in these wealthiest communities might be willing to pay exorbitant prices for homes.

In addition to examining which cities utilized the greatest percentage of jumbo mortgages and, therefore, had the greatest involvement of aggressive private bankers, I also examined which cities in America were the most aggressive in utilizing more exotic financing tools such as interest-only mortgages. If banks' aggressiveness is a major contributor to housing price increases across the country, one would expect to find that those cities that had utilized the greatest percentage of interest-only loans also have had the greatest price appreciation in homes. The percentage of interest-only loans in each city becomes a proxy of how aggressive bankers are in that region.

As expected, the statistical analysis at a 95 percent confidence level demonstrates that those cities that made the greatest use of interest-only mortgages also experienced the greatest price appreciation over the five-year period. It appears that those communities that were exposed to the greatest percentage of aggressive private bank lending indeed experienced the greatest degree of home price appreciation.

Our analysis was overly simplistic. To conduct the test correctly we would have to include many more variables that might have an influence on home prices across metropolitan areas and be certain that the newly included variables themselves were not highly correlated with each other. But as a first-blush effort, the results are encouraging. It appears that one of the reasons our wealthiest communities' homes have appreciated the most recently is that they have drawn the attention of bankers whose loose lending policies have provided the fuel to ignite a rather irrational cycle of ever-increasing home prices.

Of course, this same explanation can be used to explain the

global increase in housing prices recently. Banks worldwide have been lulled by ever greater success into lending larger and larger sums on ever more generous terms. I will return to this topic in chapter 8 when I discuss behavior of people caught in always popular Ponzi schemes.

Still, the analysis is not complete. We saw earlier that housing prices should not rise as interest rates come down if real interest rates are not changing. The true story is even worse. It turns out that, theoretically, housing prices should actually decline as inflation and nominal interest rates decrease, even if real rates remain unchanged. The reason is that during periods of high inflation, buying a house provides a very valuable tax deduction, namely, mortgage interest deductibility. Even though big nominal interest payments like 15 percent are not real, you get to deduct all of them from your taxes. In essence, you are deducting inflated unreal interest expenses from your very real earnings in determining your tax bill. The higher the inflation, the greater the value of the mortgage interest deduction. But as we've seen, in chapter 2, as inflation has eased, so has the value of this tax shield. In 1985, the mortgage deduction might have been worth as much as 30 percent of the value of a home. Today, given the lower nominal interest rate environment, this deduction is worth more like 9 percent of the value of the house. The house should have declined 20 percent in value over the period solely because inflation and interest rates have eased and this tax shield was worth less. Instead, we have witnessed a dramatic increase in house prices.

The impact of improper bank lending on residential real estate is not just limited to its impact on varying home prices over time. Bank lending practices also explain one of the "inexplicable" conundrums in stock market valuation work, why stocks go down when inflation goes up. Its impact may be even more broadly felt than that. One could construct a theory of the causes of business cycles based on this analysis. Business cycles have never been well understood, but now we see that banks' overly restrictive lending to the housing and automobile sectors during periods of high inflation might indeed take a healthy economy into recession. Similarly, during periods of low inflation, as exists today, banks' overly aggressive lending to housing may lead to bubbles and eventual bursts as they retreat from their overly aggressive lending. In their wake there will be not only disappointed homeowners, but an entire economy that will be dragged into recession because so many parts of the economy are entangled with rapidly appreciating real estate.

And so we may have found the explanation not only of overpriced homes, but also of stock market valuations and inflation and a general theory of the cause of business cycles during variable inflation periods. With that, let us turn to the individual homebuyer to see if we can understand why he might spend all this easily financed money on a home purchase.

8

Ponzi Would Be Proud

Ponzi schemes are pyramid schemes in which investors are promised extraordinary returns on their capital, but nothing productive is ever invested in. Early investors receive their returns from the cash supplied by later investors. Imagine a vertical pyramid where the earliest entrants are at the top and the base of the pyramid has to continually grow and expand in order to be able to afford to pay those above. Ponzi schemes actually exist; they are not just theoretical. But they rarely last long as it becomes increasingly difficult to make good on promised returns to such an exponentially growing population. The name comes from Charles Ponzi, who in 1920 convinced investors to turn over their life savings in exchange for small, ornate certificates that promised a 50 percent return in forty-five days. In just one month, 30,000 investors had given him some $10 million of their hard-earned money. He was arrested in August, 1920.

The danger of Ponzi schemes, and the reason they are illegal all over the world, is that they can be very enticing. Even if you suspect where the money is going, you can see that many people are actually getting rich off their investments in the scheme. Regardless of how many warnings you might receive from knowledgeable experts, you have physical evidence that the scheme seems to be working: the new cars bought by your friends, the new boats bought by your workmates, and the huge distributions of cash to those lucky enough to have gotten in early. The greatest challenge to man's rational faculties and abilities to act reasonably and listen to logical argument occurs when the evidence he sees runs counter to his logical thought. He might even delay in playing the Ponzi scheme because he feels it couldn't possibly work in the long run, only to be dragged in as the wealth acquired by his friends becomes too overwhelming to ignore.

I'm not suggesting that the entire residential housing market worldwide is one large Ponzi scheme that is certain to crash as the number of willing buyers is finally exhausted. But we need to ask the question whether there are elements of the housing market that make it ripe for Ponzi-type exploitation by some participants. Is some portion of the run-up in housing prices produced by an irrational momentum-style investing driven more by stories of great profits in the past than by strong fundamental analysis of the potential of the market going forward?

There are certainly elements of the current housing market that seem Ponzi-like. Although the housing market has been flat for a hundred years in real terms, the fact that it has appreciated nominally for the past fifty years provides the kind of profits available in a Ponzi-like scheme. The fact that homeowners comprise 70 percent of all U.S. households is also important. It means that while there is a large cost hurdle for first-time buyers, most of the population is already benefiting to some extent from the scheme. Current homeowners who want to trade up don't have to come up with any new cash; they only have to double down their equity appreciation to date. In housing, even many new first-time buyers don't have to pony up any cash, as the banks provide 100 percent of the money. The "cost" of playing is not felt until much later when buyers realize that they have signed their future earnings away in the form of a million-dollar mortgage. The game can stop, the housing prices can drop back to realistic levels, everything will return to normal, but that million-dollar mortgage will not go away. In an improvement on the typical Ponzi scheme, in the housing market you get to play now and pay later.

One prime component of a successful Ponzi scheme stands out in bold relief in the housing market. Namely, there are many home-owners who are willing to testify to having achieved astronomical returns over time on their invested capital. Interestingly, the great majority of these "profits" have not been monetized or taken off the table; they still reside in the form of equity in a succession of bigger and more expensive homes. Any poker player knows that table win-nings aren't real until you cash out and have the money in your pocket.

Even if you believed housing was overpriced, how strong would your convictions have to be to fly in the face of the "evidence" of profit potential all around you? Are you willing to sell your home to-day and realize your profit, and run the risk of missing out on more years of unusual profits? Regardless of how convincing an argument I present in this book, it is only human nature that many will ignore the logic of the argument and be swayed by the false profits being realized in the market. Who are you going to believe, me or your lying eyes?

The housing market is also perfectly suited for a Ponzi-like run because housing values are so poorly understood. If you thought it was hard to value Google's common stock when it was initially of-fered to the public, how can you put an economic price on beach-front property, city views, or inclusion in an exclusive neighborhood? Hard-to-value assets are perfect for Ponzi schemes because no price paid can be proved with certainty to be too much. This is what made the Internet stocks ideal candidates for a big unsustainable boom. Nobody had any idea what a reasonable price was. Houses are just as difficult to value.

Homeowners won't like to hear this, but their naïvete about investment valuation in general plays right in line with the Ponzis. A simple review of the reasons many people give for the housing boom, such as those presented in chapter 5, demonstrates that they have very little knowledge about how markets really work or what the real historical price data show. Most homeowners do no more pricing or valuation analysis than asking what their bank will lend them, or what a similar property sold for across the street. If markets can go completely Ponzi on you, then depending on market-based appraisals is self-defeating.

At some level Ponzi schemes have to be corrupt. Either the organizer or the supporters or the lax regulator has less than good intentions with regard to protecting the asset wealth of their fellow citizens. If you are trying to sell to a greater fool before the market crashes, with no regard for how he recovers his investment, you are part of the moral problem. If you are a real estate professional who is pushing a personal profit agenda rather than providing the best advice to your clients, you are part of the moral problem. And if you work for the Congress, or the Federal Reserve, or the FDIC and you are avoiding cracking down on the overly aggressive banks, Fannie Mae and Freddie Mac because they are contributors to your campaign or you want to protect the banks and risk harming the general electorate—you are a big part of the moral problem. If you are a regulator who honestly believes markets don't need effective regulation to work, you may not be morally deficient, but you really ought to get out more.

The timing of this housing bubble also couldn't be better for a Ponzi scheme. We live in a casino society in which profits are being created with great risk but not much hard physical effort. The third most watched sport on television is poker, which I did not even realize was a sport. Celebrities are admired not for their hard work or their knowledge but for having achieved some level of fame based more on image than substance.

The central question, and the key difference between a casino economy and a healthy productive economy, is whether anything of real value is being created in the process. If all that is happening is the shuffling of assets around the board, it is hard to see how value is being created. The Wall Street trader does create value by improving the efficiency and the cost with which trading can be accomplished. The small day trader is just pushing paper around. Economists can argue whether anything productive is happening in Las Vegas. Clearly, animal urges and addictions are being fed, but it is hard to argue that the world is one dollar better off after someone spends a long weekend in Vegas.

Is housing a real, productive market, or a casino-like roulette game? If all we are doing is shuffling assets back and forth, it is hard to argue that any great value is being created. And if we are spending enormous sums on unnecessary home enhancements, then a great deal of our investment capital is going to increasing consumption to the detriment of real, meaningful, productive investment.

It is not a coincidence that the housing bubble followed the bursting of the dot.com bubble. Assets shifted from the stock market to the housing market, but more importantly, Ponzi-like behavior shifted as well. In the 1990s, during the dot.com bubble, people got comfortable with the idea that great wealth could be created with very little real effort or knowledge. Rather than learning their lesson when the Internet stocks crashed, people seemed thrilled to move to the housing market and continue their money-shuffling ways.

Another component of perfect timing for Ponzi-like behavior is the fact that inflation has been burned out of the world economy for the first time in history. Never before have people witnessed interest rates declining by 10 to 15 percent, and they really don't know how to react. Stock market players may or may not be smart enough to know the difference between real and nominal interest rates, but I know your average home buyer isn't. Ponzi schemes require times when valuations are uncertain so as to maintain some degree of assumed reasonableness as prices escalate. The recent decline of interest rates and the reduction in inflation has added just the needed confusion to the investment picture.

Let's look at the evidence of what home prices have done recently to see if they fit a Ponzi-like explanation. Just because housing prices are high, they aren't necessarily being driven by Ponzi- or herdlike behavior. But just as we previously asked whether rational explanations were sufficient to justify today's price levels, let us ask the opposite question. Is there something in the pattern of home prices that might suggest a Ponzi-like buying spree?

Remember that the greatest recent price appreciation has occurred in our biggest cities and our swankiest communities. Residents of our biggest cities are generally our better-educated citizens, but are they our most independent thinkers? Maybe they are all ambitiously following similar life dreams, making herdlike behavior easier. Certainly, city dwellers understand that asset values can sometimes be ephemeral. Their own careers are mostly in service industries, and many have started providing these services over the Internet, the ultimate in ephemeral value. To the extent that city dwellers would be more comfortable paying high prices for softer assets, they might be more willing to pay up for land values, neighborhood considerations, and other soft values in today's home market. I don't know if the stereotype holds any longer, but the middle of our country was always considered to be more grounded, more skeptical, and more conservative. Such qualities usually don't play well to a Ponzi scheme promoter.

We have seen that housing appreciation is not limited to the United States. While it seems unlikely that the entire world could be caught up in a Ponzi scheme, it is interesting to note the similarities between homebuyers in Ireland, Australia, or Britain when they talk about their expectations of the market. Until just this year, many of these buyers sounded very similar when they estimated future expected growth rates of housing that were usually in the double digits and completely unsustainable in the long run. Similarly, all three countries had a large portion of their population playing the housing market for purely speculative investment purposes. Maybe they are not all playing the exact same Ponzi game, but there are indications that they are all playing something similar. The biggest price gainers overseas have been in the biggest cities, where aggressive yuppies and bankers live.

Even the fact that the real price increase in homes has accelerated in the last nine years fits well with a Ponzi explanation. The reason is that the Internet bubble started disintegrating two years after that, and housing was a logical place for Ponzi players to shift their assets and continue their game.

I don't mean to suggest that the only reason for the housing bubble is a worldwide Ponzi scheme. But market economists do their analysis a disservice if they totally ignore the possible behavioral effects of herdlike investing. There have been too many examples in history of how markets have the potential of getting too "frothy," to borrow a term from Mr. Greenspan. If sellers and homebuilders are realizing extraordinary profits, buyers must be paying extraordinary prices. If they are hoping for greater fools to pay even higher prices in the future they may get caught in the deceitful web of Ponzi.

9

The Desire for Status

We have seen that there is a great deal of very loose credit available to homebuyers in the mortgage market. The incomes and wealth of our richest citizens have risen considerably over the last twenty-five years. But this does not explain why an individual homebuyer would feel compelled to spend exorbitant amounts of money on his home. Just because the money is available does not mean that it has to be spent. And, of course, funds spent on housing are necessary funds not available for other pursuits and interests.

Perhaps homebuyers are just irrational. Unlike a sophisticated financial market in which arbitrage opportunities assure a degree of rationality in the pricing of assets, there is no such guarantee that individual home purchasers will act rationally. Certainly, the housing market is a big market, but that doesn't guarantee that its prices are correct. Unlike a financial market, the housing market is a real market with real hard assets—houses. It is much more difficult to arbitrage profits out of single investor errors in a real market like housing than in a financial market where deep trading in securities and derivatives allow effortless and substantial long and short positions.

What is there to prevent a homebuyer from overpaying for his house? Now that you really understand how home purchases are financed, you might conclude that overpaying is the norm. Most homebuyers are infrequent participants in the housing market and therefore are reliant on real estate agents and other supposed experts for valuation advice. Most people don't have a clue to how much they can afford to spend on a home; they leave it to the experts at the bank to determine the amount they should spend. If people really do spend on a home all the money they qualify for at the bank, then the bank becomes the limiting factor in determining prices. As we saw in chapter 7, much of the empirical statistics strongly support the view that the banks and their lending formulas are indeed the driving force behind this price boom.

It is not just the banks that the homebuyer turns to for expert advice. The real estate agent he hires is motivated, not to get him to bid low, but to bid high. The real estate agency business is very competitive, and the agent only gets paid if he closes the deal. The appraiser is introduced into the process to provide some moderating influence, but he also is paid only if his numbers support the deal price. The appraiser might ask the real estate agent to bring him other overpriced deals in the neighborhood that he can put in his comparables list to justify the high price being paid. There is no motivation to achieve a realistic level of valuation in the neighborhood, only an effort to garner the highest valuation possible.

Possibly the greatest disservice the appraiser does is inflating the relevant values by focusing solely on comparable "market" transactions. Nowhere in his analysis is there a reference to what prices have done historically, what they are in comparable neighborhoods in other cities and other countries, or what the raw land is worth if put to other uses. No, his total emphasis is on measuring what occurred most recently in the local market in comparable housing sales. If the market is rational and always achieves reasonable pricing, this is an adequate approach. But it can be self-reinforcing if real markets like housing have a tendency to inflate and run away with themselves. If they do, what sense does it make for an expert to opine that a price paid is reasonable when compared to the most recent crazy price paid for similar properties in the community?

It's reasonable to assume that even though the housing market is not as efficient as a big, sophisticated financial market like the New York Stock Exchange, it, like any free market, will certainly reward smart players and punish dumb participants in the long run. It is this self-regulating nature of free markets that make capitalism so powerful a force for growth and wealth creation.

But housing and mortgage markets are uniquely different from most other markets for goods and services. They deal in very long-lived assets, namely thirty-year mortgages and hundred-year homes. It is the nature of participants in markets for very long-lived assets that they often do a poor job of pricing risk in the short term. The reason, of course, is that risks to these long-lived assets usually comes in one bundle, all at once, and very infrequently. Sure, housing will suffer if interest rates move back up to 10 percent, but what are the odds of that? Do homebuyers really plan well for possible job losses, economic downturns, and medical emergencies that might drain their cash reserves? Do banks really understand their exposure if housing prices should decline 30 percent nationwide? Other long-lived asset industries have exactly this same problem, which helps explain why insurance companies are never adequately capitalized for once-in-a-century floods and why airlines always seem to go bankrupt when oil prices spike up.

So if we currently have a bubble in real estate, those homebuyers who are overpaying for homes and those banks that are aggressively financing them have not paid yet for their mistakes. In fact, they have been rewarded. They have enjoyed ever-greater profits riding what is an unsustainable wave of ever-increasing home prices. In an irrational world it is the dumbest players who make the most money. How do you convince someone to be more rational when irrationality pays so well?

In addition to overrelying on supposed experts and the correctness of the market, homebuyers, like the banks, appear to fixate their analysis of housing affordability on the first-year ratios of coverage of mortgage interest and principal. We have seen the banks push them toward this shortsighted analysis, but it is somewhat surprising that homebuyers fall for it. Homebuyers today seem very comfortable purchasing homes at prices that require 40 percent of their combined salaries going forward, even if this means that 90 percent of their disposable income goes to the house. They don't seem to perform adequate what-if analyses of higher interest rates and lower incomes in the future. Most importantly, they don't focus adequate attention on the sheer size of the mortgage note they sign at closing.

In today's environment of low interest rates it is possible to acquire a home by pledging both your and your spouse's income for the foreseeable future. In chapter 7, we saw that in a high inflation environment, we would only pay less than three times our combined income for a home. Thanks to lower rates and the creative financing vehicles available today we can pay 10 to 12 times our income for a home purchase. Because nominal interest rates are lower, the deals look very similar to us in the first year when viewed from the perspective of a cash flow coverage of interest.

But there is a very important difference between these two transactions. In the first case, in a high inflation, high interest rate environment, the buyer ends up with a mortgage equal to about 2.5 times his combined income, in the second case, a low inflation, low interest rate environment, he ends up signing a mortgage note equal to 10 to 11 times his combined income. And in the current low inflation environment, he is not going to have general inflation around to pop his salary and help him work his way out of this debt. This is real debt. It is attached to the home, but if the home is sold at a loss, it doesn't magically disappear. It will follow him everywhere for the rest of his life.

A clear proof that many home purchasers do not focus on the total size of the mortgage note they sign is demonstrated by reviewing how many mortgage bankers bill their fees. For competitive reasons, many advertise "no fee" mortgages. And most homebuyers are smart enough to realize that they are being had if they have to pay additional, previously unmentioned fees in cash at the closing. It is hard for a banker to change the agreed-upon interest rate on the loan, although some will try, using arguments about the borrower's poor credit quality and credit reporting history to do just that.

How, then, do the mortgage bankers exact fees? They simply add them to the back-end mortgage amount that the homebuyer owes. They then take the present value of these additional homeowner costs out of the deal up front by selling the mortgage note to a bank. The naïve homebuyer is happy, as he doesn't owe any additional cash at closing and is too ignorant to ask about the size of the mortgage note he is signing.

This not only occurs in new home sales but in many refinancings. People who owe $300,000 on a home end up refinancing their mortgage to take advantage of lower rates, but because they don't focus on the amount of the note they sign, they can end up owing much more than $300,000 on the new note. And this is in cases where they take no money out of the refinancing for their own purposes.

So in a world of declining interest rates and loose bank credit, home prices can reach rather extravagant levels if homebuyers are fairly indifferent to the size of the mortgage notes they sign. Imagine that the seller, rather than asking you to sign a million-dollar promissory note to buy a home, demanded you come up with the money in cash from your savings. Would you proceed with the home purchase knowing that you had to sell two cars, raid your children's college fund, and cash out most of your retirement savings to do it? Humans always seem quicker to spend money that they do not identify as their own—which is not the definition of perfect economic rationality.

But homebuyers are not complete idiots. They know how many zeroes there are in the number 1,000,000. Even if the system is geared toward getting them to spend ever-increasing sums on their housing, surely we cannot attribute their cavalier behavior to just being fooled by savvy bankers and brokers. People can't just be tricked into borrowing millions of dollars only to give it away at closing. (A typical house closing today consists of you acquiring a place of shelter in exchange for you and your spouse signing a legal agreement, the mortgage note, that will put you and your spouse in legal servitude for the foreseeable future.)

There must be some real reason why homebuyers are willing to spend millions of dollars solely to put a roof over their heads. The wealthy might be excused from this discussion, since their spending big money on a house does not create any additional hardship to them and does not prevent them from pursuing any other lifestyle choices they might have. They are not cash-constrained when it comes to making consumption choices. But what about the middle and upper-middle classes? Why are they willing to subject themselves to the anxiety of trying to make each month for years into the future a mortgage payment that represents a huge percentage of their take-home pay? And why have they made an apparently conscious decision to spend a significantly greater amount of their income on housing and a significantly smaller amount on vacations, travel, new business opportunities, charitable causes, child support, educational opportunities, entertainment plans, and the general welfare of their families and their communities? Not to put too fine a point on it, but if more people were willing to scrape by and live in a modest $500,000 home instead of insisting on a $1 million home, they would free up $500,000 to help the poor, cure the sick, care for the elderly, house the homeless, educate the masses, and feed the starving. Obviously, just throwing money at these massive world problems will not cure them, but well-thought-out plans to stimulate growth and build better institutions still require money. What is it that drives people to obvious and unfettered consumption in their home purchases when that capital could do so much good if employed elsewhere?

To answer this question, it is helpful to break down the benefits of home ownership into four categories: pure shelter cost, the cost of local economic participation, the amenity value, and the status value.

Imagine a house in San Francisco that has just been bought for $800,000, which happens to be the average home price there now. Of that total price it is hard to imagine that the buyers are spending more than $100,000 for simple shelter from the elements, inasmuch as a simple small home could easily be built in another town that would provide adequate shelter. Perhaps an additional $200,000 could be justified if by living in San Francisco they find economic opportunities (perhaps in Silicon Valley) unavailable in other cities, although it is not clear why they couldn't just rent rather than own and so capture this premium.

What are the amenities of San Francisco worth? Are they such that the couple would bid up the local home purchase price? Is it worth a $100,000 premium to be close to restaurants they enjoy? Is it worth another $100,000 premium to be close to the San Francisco Opera? What is a nice view of the bay worth?

Regardless of what you pile on, it's hard to get to the average San Francisco home prices solely by measuring the value of rational benefits and amenities. And that says nothing about trying to explain the $5 million to $20 million homes located there. Is there some other component or benefit that a person might garner by purchasing a home in San Francisco? And could it be large enough to explain a $500,000 difference between the cost of housing in San Francisco and other cities in the country?

My answer is that individuals' quest for status might explain it all. There are goods that economists have often referred to as luxury or status goods because some people feel compelled to buy more of them even as their price increases. People seem to have identified diamonds and jewels and motor yachts as products that they don't mind paying exorbitant prices for because that is part of the status game. The fact that the price is ridiculous signals that the owner has plenty of money and power and status, and the high price also prevents status imposters from making the same acquisition. Under this model, the higher the price, the more exclusive the purchase and the greater status achieved. The fact that status demand might increase as prices make the product more "exclusive" means that traditional economic supply and demand analysis does not apply.

While people are familiar with $10,000 designer dresses and million-dollar automobiles, we usually don't think of housing as a status item. But what started out as simple shelter, as recently as our parents' generation, now often has a status element attached to it, reflected in its size, its amenities, and the neighborhood and city in which it is located. If you doubt this, think about a home purchase you have made or heard of recently. Was the home purchased because it had an adequate number of bedrooms for the people living there? Was it highly valued because it was in the right school district? Or was a high price paid because it was in the right community or had the right zip code? Did the real estate agent point out celebrities that lived nearby? Did you check out the view instead of the water pressure in the shower? What was the real reason for insisting on a five-acre plot instead of one acre? Were you more concerned that you would like the place or that your guests would?

I originally thought of the idea of the importance of status to housing when I reviewed the list of cities worldwide that were experiencing the fastest appreciation in housing prices and the greatest divergence from rental values. Miami Beach. San Francisco. New York City. Paris. London. Aspen. Nice. Las Vegas. Madrid. Saint-Tropez. These are some of the wealthiest and most exclusive communities in the world. Remember, this is not a list of the most expensive places to live, rather it is a list of cities in which home prices have appreciated the most recently. I started to investigate whether status could have a meaningful impact on home prices and whether the result would be limited to only our richest cities.

The cities with the fastest appreciating home prices are those in which residents put an unusually high degree of emphasis on status. The anonymity of large cities pushes people to find ways to differentiate themselves, and these large cities seem to attract ambitious people for which success and status is extremely important. So do some high-end resort communities.

It also partially explains why the cities and neighborhoods with the most expensive houses have witnessed the greatest appreciation recently. The whole idea of status is exclusivity. If a community isn't exclusive, it can't confer status. And the best way to create exclusivity is to raise prices. Only the rich need apply.

It turns out my theory of status also dovetails quite well with Glaeser's and Gyourko's work on restrictive zoning and housing prices. The communities with the greatest zoning restrictions are trying to create exclusivity, the key to status.

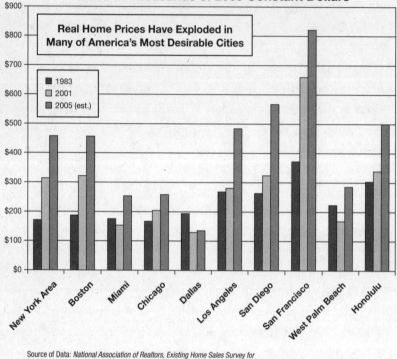

Figure 9.1: Real Home Prices After Adjusting for Inflation in Some of America's Most Desirable Cities in Thousands of 2005 Constant Dollars

Real Home Prices Have Exploded in Many of America's Most Desirable Cities

Legend:
- 1983
- 2001
- 2005 (est.)

Source of Data: *National Association of Realtors, Existing Home Sales Survey for Home Prices,* and *Bureau of Labor Statistics*

But that doesn't explain why purchase prices in these exclusive cities have gotten so out of line with rentals. Or does it? If you rent in one of these wealthy communities, are you really part of the community? Do renters get invited to join the golf club? Maybe the disparity between rents and purchase costs is the best indicator that status is indeed playing a large part in setting house prices in these exclusive communities.

And a status theory of housing values explains why the most costly homes and the greatest price appreciation has occurred in our major cities and not out in rural areas. What good is buying a luxury home if no one is there to see you in it? Just as an unobserved tree falling in the forest makes no noise, a big beautiful home out in the lonely woods does little to increase status. The key to appreciating status is to have an audience—and there is no bigger audience than that of our major cities and the playgrounds of their wealthiest residents.

Finally, status can also explain the international component of the housing boom, as status seeking is not an exclusively American pastime. Sure enough, the cities that have seen the fastest escalation in housing prices worldwide are the homes of the rich and famous. And within each city, the neighborhoods that have the fastest-growing prices are the ritziest and priciest.

Let's test our hypothesis that status seeking is driving home prices worldwide. We need to try to isolate what portion of a home purchase price is due to status seeking. Or we need to be able to determine if those cities that have the highest home price appreciation recently also place the highest value on status. Again we need a way to measure status value. Let's look at other expensive item purchases. Is there a way to separate out the premium one pays for a Ferrari and see how much is paid for the car's performance characteristics and how much is being paid to increase one's status by either being seen driving it or parking it in your driveway?

It seems reasonable to assume that if two condominium apartments on the top two floors in a high-rise building share exactly the same floor plan, the same views, and the same roof decks and access, then any price premium paid for the penthouse as opposed to the floor directly under it would have to be chalked up to status. And we know that this price difference can be very large, often representing 20 to 50 percent of the total value of the penthouse. Penthouses are ideal status goods because no one can have a higher condo in a building than the penthouse.

Similarly, one often sees a substantial premium paid for brand-new luxury cars on the showroom floor as opposed to those sold used that have been only one day off the lot. If they have the same warranty protection it might be interesting to see how this premium varies by city. Down-to-earth Midwest drivers who don't give a lick about status would probably assign a very small discount to the slightly "used" vehicle while more status-conscious types in the big cities on our coasts might indeed pay quite a premium in order to brag about their "new" car purchase.

There is much anecdotal evidence that people will pay a premium to live right on the coast as opposed to being a block from the ocean. Here the view and beach access is important, but it is also very important to be able to show your friends that you can't get closer to the water without a snorkel. Perhaps this is why coastline properties have recently risen in price the most. I think there is also a status component to paying high prices for condos with spectacular views, as I believe many owners rarely take advantage of the view themselves but always point it out when their status-determining friends come to visit.

If I am right that status drives home prices, then in order for real house prices to have increased in price exponentially recently there must have been an increase in the importance of status over time. If we remember our parents' lives and where they chose to retire, and compared it to our own and ours friends' status-conscious lives, I think there is a solid argument that status is not only more important today than it used to be, but that its importance is growing.

If it is true that status is becoming ever more important, it might explain some of the unexplainable increase in value that homes have exhibited recently. Of course, status seeking itself is not completely rational and economic and productive, so at best we may have just found a name for the buyer's irrationality. We will say more about this later in this chapter.

If housing is increasing in value because of an increased emphasis on status in our society, then the price of other status goods should also be appreciating rapidly. In addition, our society should be spending more time celebrating celebrity, which appears to be the case if you have turned on television recently or read a popular magazine.

Table 9.2 shows the price changes in some selected status goods.

Table 9.2 Nominal Price Appreciation of a Number of Selected Status Goods Compared to Median Existing Home Price Appreciation

Status Item	1976	2004	1976–2004 Multiple Increase
Prep School, Groton, one-year tuition, room, board	$4,200	$35,800	8.5X
University/Harvard, one-year tuition, room, board, insurance	$5,900	$39,880	6.8X
Opera/Two season tickets, Metropolitan Opera, Saturday night, box	$480	$4,720	9.8X
Champagne/Dom Perignon, case, Sherry-Lehmann, NYC	$300	$1,439	4.8X
Dinner/La Tour d'Argent/Paris, estimated per person	$34	$331	9.7X
Hotel/Two-bedroom suite, park view, The Stanhope, NYC	$333	$1,235	3.7X
Motor Yacht/Hatteras 75'	$214,700	$4,500,000	21.0X
Sailing Yacht/Nautor's Swan '68	$384,300	$3,864,654	10.1X
Airplane/Learjet 31A, standard equipment, certified, ten passengers	$1,800,000	$8,240,000	4.6X
Helicopter/Sikorsky S-76C+, full executive options	$1,300,000	$9,000,000	6.9X
Automobile/Rolls-Royce Silver Seraph	$38,000	$328,750	8.7X
Overall CPI Index	56.90	188.90	3.3X
Existing Home Sales	$38,100	$208,000	5.5X

Source of Data: Forbes Magazine. Analysis: Author

As can be seen in the table, home prices increasing fivefold over this thirty-year period no longer look unusual when compared to other goods status seekers seek. Startlingly, seventy-five-foot yachts have increased 21 times in value in thirty years. Certainly, they are much better equipped today, so the price multiple overstates their true economic appreciation. But it now takes a 400-foot yacht to grab the attention of the world yachting community, and some yacht clubs won't even take boats as small as seventy-five feet. The biggest personal yachts today cost over $250 million to build, which puts the $4.5 million Hatteras in Table 9.2 to shame. Therefore, maybe this table understates the appreciation of true status in these catagories.

If only the very wealthy were concerned about status it would not present a problem to the housing market. The wealthy have made a conscious decision to move investment assets out of the stock market and into real estate. For the rich, buying housing properties is no longer a game of leveraging incomes but instead is an investment allocation issue. If home prices come down, it won't be because the wealthy are unable to meet a mortgage payment.

The very wealthy in America have done very well for themselves over the last twenty-five years. But they still represent a small percentage of all Americans. Most of the income gains recently have gone to the top 10 percent of Americans, and most of that has gone to the top 1 percent.

That still leaves 80 to 90 million American households that depend on their salaries to afford the monthly mortgage payment. These are the people who, if stretched on a home purchase, could have real trouble meeting their obligations in the future, especially if they experience job losses, divorces, or a medical emergencies.

It is for this middle and upper-middle income segment of the population that status seeking becomes a risky game, especially with regard to buying homes. It even has a cliché associated with it: keeping up with the Joneses. Housing provides an ideal vehicle for these social climbers who are determined to move on up.

Housing is unique among status goods because it is not only a very large purchase, often five time to eight times salary level, but it can be almost self-financing. In a wonderful new academic paper in the April 2005 issue of the *Journal of Political Economy*, Gary Becker and Kevin Murphy of the University of Chicago and Ivan Werning of the Massachusetts Institute of Technology argue that status seekers are drawn to risky lottery-type investments with small initial investments but big potential upsides. Even if the economic odds are against them, status seekers like these types of plays because if they win they have the potential to jump up to an entirely new status class. There is no traditional investment yielding 10 to 15 percent that is going to give a poor person investing a couple of hundred bucks the opportunity to skip up the status ladder. Lotteries are attractive, even though the odds are long, because if they win $5 into $10 million they have won the status sweepstakes. The authors make a wonderful contribution to the literature by identifying the fact that the status seeker's objective is not to just get a positive return on their investment, but to make a quantum leap in their returns and thus enter a new class. And it looks like many people will undertake "bad" investments like lotteries just to have the chance to hit it big and increase their status.

The authors do not discuss housing, but what better way for someone of modest means to really have a chance at "making it" and escaping his class? Here is a status seeker's ideal investment. No money down, a big deal, a quick return, lots of volatility, and banks that will let almost anyone play with lots of the house's money. It is as if you showed up in Vegas broke and depressed and the casino put you at the heavy hitters' table and loaned you the chips to play with.

So the overpriced housing market is not only going to attract status seekers because they want to change their neighborhood and hang out with a better crowd, it is going to attract status seekers because they are willing to make a bad economic bet in hopes of winning and leaping up in class and status. Housing investors may pretend to listen to housing bubble warnings, but they can't wait to get back to double down their equity profits from their last house sale into a bigger and nicer and pricier new home.

While this type of gambling behavior could easily become addictive, addictions are not necessary to explain the status-seeking homebuyer. He is in it for the big hit. Mere 20 percent returns don't interest him. He needs to triple his investment and then do it again and again to be able to attain the status he thinks he is deserving of.

This type of behavior is extremely unstable if it becomes widespread in a market like housing. Not only are middle-income status seekers making uneconomic bets trying to hit the jackpot, but these same people are playing beyond their means. That is the only explanation for why ARM issuance grew to 37 percent of the total new mortgage market and exceeded 70 percent in many cities in California during a period of record-low long-term interest rates. Buyers, probably status seekers, were stretching to buy the nicest home they could afford, didn't mind taking on the additional risk of not locking in rates, and even planned to flip the property before the first mortgage reset period in three to five years and move up again. The problem is that if a majority of the buyers are acting so recklessly, it is only a matter of time until an economic downturn, an interest rate increase, or a housing downturn disrupts their highly leveraged plans.

Is the housing market more secure and stable if we call the buyers status seekers rather than irrational investors? Possibly. But probably not that much more secure or stable. Even though status seekers have been around since the dawn of time and status seeking may be an innate force in not only humans but many species of animals, there is little that is productive or good about it. It is hard to call status seeking economically productive. Certainly it makes the seeker happier, just as consuming alcoholic beverages makes one genetically prone to alcoholism "happier," but little social good comes from from it. Economic activity, trade, and productivity improvements are considered good because they increase the amount of goods and services that can be distributed to the populace. What good does status seeking create? And if it is only a warm and fuzzy feeling internal to the status seeker, how does it translate into the real economic progress we need to provide for all of the world's people.

Clearly, if people have a sudden moral awakening and realize that life has more to offer than a never-ending race to consume more than a neighbor, housing prices in the ritziest neighborhoods could come under pressure. But we don't have to wait for such a moral epiphany. Because paying big prices for houses solely to acquire status is economically unproductive, buyers will not be able to recoup their investments in rental incomes. Banks will eventually pull the plug on this type of lottery-like status seeking, so the housing market will crash regardless of whether status seekers mend their ways. And many of the most stretched status seekers will exhaust their incomes long before they ever become satisfied with the size of their homes or the look of their neighbors.

10

The Morning After

There are very strong indications that the global housing boom is finally over. Japan crashed in the 1990s, Australia turned down in 2004. Britain seemed to have peaked in 2005, and there are rumblings in America that prices and sales volumes are now beginning to fall.

Industry experts have tried to predict what the post-boom era will look like. Their predictions are as unreasonably optimistic as they were during the boom. These experts suggest that if there is a decline, it will be regional in nature, only affect the most overpriced cities, not unduly impact the U.S. economy, and will be more of a soft landing than a total collapse. They universally agree that home prices will continue to grow at 4 to 6 percent in the future.

That is one scenario. But that is not the most likely scenario. Prices have gone up too much in too many areas for there not to be a major correction that will be national, or possibly global, and that will have a very meaningful impact on the world economy.

Even those who argue that the impact will be limited to the most overpriced cities fail to see that these very overpriced cities are also our largest cities with the highest aggregate values of real estate. The twenty-two most overpriced cities represent more than 40 percent of the total value of all residential real estate in the country. Even if a housing correction were somehow magically constrained within their city limits, the negative wealth effects would be felt countrywide.

While the most expensive homes in the most expensive cities may suffer the greatest declines in a housing price downturn, there are many good reasons why the carnage will not be contained in just these exclusive neighborhoods.

Consider how homebuilders have been making profits lately. They have been building on the outskirts of moderately priced cities where land is readily available and their equipment can get in and out easily. While building a single house in an exclusive wealthy enclave might be profitable, big homebuilders like to build hundreds of homes at once, something they are incapable of doing inside well-established neighborhoods. As we have seen, homebuilders are mainly sellers and not buyers of housing, but their business will suffer tremendously when the housing market turns because of the locations where they operate.

They do not typically want to get involved in wealthy areas where a large amount of their capital will be tied up during construction in high land costs. Rather they do most of their building on the frontiers of more moderately priced cities. And when the housing market turns, these frontier communities will also suffer.

In the real estate downturn of the 1990s, many American cities were busy building second and third ring roads at greater distances from their city centers. Houses that were farthest from downtown on these partially completed highways suffered the most when prices declined. Similarly, when housing prices decline this time around, it will be the new construction on the edge of towns that will suffer, as people will no longer have to trade off longer commute times to save money on housing.

This is the primary reason that homebuilders' stocks will suffer during a housing downturn. There will still be a need for them to provide inexpensive new housing, but they will be unable to find sufficient land close enough to city centers to compete with existing home prices in the area that will be dropping. The exception, of course, are high-rises that will continue to be built in coastal areas that allow them to take advantage of the large premium buyers who are willing to pay to be near the water. San Diego and Miami high-rise construction might slow, but in the long term, building up is the arbitrage solution to the high land prices that have been established in this boom, and high-rise condominium construction will continue on both coasts.

So the first fallout from a pricing decline in the wealthiest neighborhoods will be a reduction of new home construction and sales on the periphery of these neighborhoods and cities. Secondly, while the wealthy may have additional resources that prevent them from losing their homes to foreclosure in a downturn, those status-seeking young couples trying desperately to keep up with the Joneses by buying homes beyond their means will really get squeezed. Many million-dollar homes will face foreclosure as overleveraged owners realize that the economics work better with the property dead rather than alive. People will realize that they can't afford high mortgage payments during tough economic times and will see in a world of depressed real estate prices that it makes more sense to default to the bank than sell the property and realize less than the balance on the mortgage.

So wealthy neighborhoods will suffer losses as those stretched are forced to default and banks repossess and cause forced auctions in the market. The rich will suffer equally on paper but will most likely avoid losing their homes, as they will continue to make their mortgage payments, if they have any, even if they have to eat into their savings to do it.

The secondary impact from the biggest and wealthiest cities undergoing a correction may be even larger than the damage in the wealthy enclaves themselves. Real estate downturns always hit harder in the more middle-class neighborhoods because it is these people who are dependent on a healthy economy and job outlook to make their monthly mortgage payments. Look at Los Angeles and San Diego. The real fallout from a housing correction will be felt hours away in San Bernardino and Riverside as many middle-income residents of San Diego and LA look miles inland in search of more reasonably priced homes. The lucky ones reinvested the profits they made in the sale of their LA and San Diego homes, and so their losses will likely be limited to giving back the paper profits they made during the boom. But many will suffer real losses when housing collapses in these inland areas because it no longer will be necessary to commute hundreds of miles in order to work in San Diego or Los Angeles.

There is another secondary effect that will cause even greater damage than the initial shock felt by the overpriced wealthy epicenter of the coming housing collapse. The economy will take a very big hit from the housing collapse, and the fallout from the economic retrenchment will hit our more modest communities the hardest. Although the Midwest and the interior states have not enjoyed anywhere near the home price appreciation of our coastal cities, they will still face severe housing price risk as the weakened economy shakes through their towns. These are poorer communities to begin with. Many have been losing population, they are not as plugged into the global economy as our coastal cities are, and their manufacturing prowess has been in a long decline. Once accelerated job losses associated with the end of the housing boom hit these more traditional American towns, their home prices will drop violently downward. A $125,000 house in the Midwest that has appreciated $20,000 in the last nine years has as big a percentage risk of a decline in price as a three million dollar home in Malibu. When moderate income cities get hit with a bad economy and a weak housing market, people miss mortgage payments, banks foreclose, and then prices really fall. As I said earlier, if home prices have not grown tremendously in your town because of lots of new home construction, this increase in supply may act to severely depress prices once the artificial demand is lessened and the easy mortgage money dries up. Houses do not have to go up in price in order to come down. The prices of many homes in the Midwest will end up lower than they were before the boom.

How big will the impact of a housing retrenchment be on the general economy? Enormous! People have mistakenly tried to compare a national housing collapse to a bear market in stocks. There is no comparison. The U.S. stock market in total is worth some $15 trillion. Residential real estate in America is now valued at more than $20 trillion. And that is not the only difference. More than 75 percent of all U.S. stocks held by individuals are held by the richest 10 percent of the population. Nearly 70 percent of Americans own their own homes. A housing decline will be felt much more broadly.

While historically stocks are more volatile in price than housing, housing is typically purchased with significantly more debt leverage. A typical home is purchased with 80 to 90 percent debt. The total margin debt relative to the value of all stocks is less than 5 percent. This means that the net effect on investor wealth is five to ten times higher for a similar housing price percentage decline as compared to a stock decline. If you have 80 percent debt on your home and the market price drops 10 percent, you have just absorbed a 50 percent drop in the value of your equity. (Try it. Assume a $400,000 mortgage on a $500,000 house with initial equity of $100,000. If the price drops to $450,000, the equity is suddenly only $50,000.)

Even homeowners with less leverage in their home who feel relatively safe from a housing price decline should take care. If you had 40 percent equity in your house and the market price drops 30 percent you will see 75 percent of your total equity wiped out.

Imagine a stock market decline so substantial that 50 to 100 percent of many investors' net worth evaporated. It has never happened, not even during the market crash of 1929. If housing declines in price by 30 percent, which is simply a return to where prices were in many cities just two years ago, many people would lose most or all of their net worth. Economists talk about the wealth effects when homeowners feel "slightly" poorer if housing prices adjust a little. Nobody is talking about the correct magnitudes of this possible disaster. Prices could easily return to where they were seven to nine years ago. For those big cities that have seen the biggest home price appreciations recently, this would mean a decline in home values of approximately 50 to 60 percent. Such a large price adjustment would wipe out almost everyone's total home equity. It is silly to talk about what the wealth effect on GDP might be in such a scenario since lots of people wouldn't have any wealth left to talk about.

It is important to highlight these worst-case scenarios because most of the media discussion to date about the ramifications of a housing decline has been driven by very optimistic scenarios that involve slight price downturns and predictions of soft landings or pauses in a continually increasing market. If we begin to understand the risks involved on the downside, we will begin to dedicate the resources and attention we need to try to avert a real disaster.

The major impact of an adjustment in housing prices on the economy is not going to be due to the wealth effect. It will result from the simple fact that our economy for at least five years has been built on only two foundations, the housing market and government (mainly military) spending.

I firmly believe that had it not been for the housing boom, the U.S. economy would have contracted over the last five years. Economists generally underestimate both the impact of the housing boom on GDP growth historically and the effect a housing price decline might have.

The first and obvious economic impact is that about a million real estate brokers who have been chasing 6 percent commissions on million-dollar homes with lottery-like enthusiasm will immediately become unemployed. Next, there are at least a million more people who work as mortgage bankers, appraisers, title lawyers, commercial bankers, and mortgage packagers who are also going to have to dust off their résumés.

It is hard to estimate percentages, but one would expect the mortgage business to slow by at least 60 percent in a downturn and the brokerage business to fall by a similar amount. If prices drop 30 percent and volume of sales is off by half, real estate commissions paid will be reduced by 65 percent, and that assumes that the realtors' fee commission schedule holds at current percentages.

The economic impact of a housing price decline is not limited to the real estate agent and mortgage community. The next business that will dry up is the renovation business. Owners will have no motivation to renovate the kitchen or add another bathroom if their home is worth less than they paid for it. New home construction will also almost cease. In effect, homebuilders have built out any land they can find that they can make a profit on at the boom level of prices.

If prices adjust downward 30 to 40 percent there will be no more projects that make sense.

The construction industry, the home renovation industry, the banking industry, and the real estate industry are four of the largest industries in America. Layoffs in these industries will be significant enough to cause a major recession. But, unfortunately, the story is not over.

Free market economies suffer ripple effects. When Suzie Realtor gets laid off, she buys less groceries, attends fewer movies, buys fewer dresses, takes fewer vacations, buys a new car less frequently, and eats out less often. Thus, the economic impact is not going to be limited to a few of our largest industries. The pullback in consumption from those who face reduced salaries and layoffs in the housing industry will pull other healthy industries down with them. Layoffs will spread, and the economy will begin a serious contraction.

We have already seen that the housing bubble is not limited to the United States. Other countries facing bubble-like real estate prices will begin their contraction. Because the United States is such a driving force of the world's total overall consumption, a recession here is sure to spread globally. There is no world power that can replace the purchasing power that might evaporate in the United States. So, the recession that starts here will be the force that ends up deflating the housing bubbles worldwide. Global recessions will result. No country will escape, as even developing countries that have no housing bubble will suffer mightily once domestic economic growth turns negative. The first rule of developing country economics is, No U.S. growth, no U.S. consumer demand, no developing country growth. Thanks to globalization we are all in this together.

If you are squeamish perhaps you should stop reading here, for I have not told you the worst part. Remember that significant amount of debt leverage that homeowners have on their homes that magnifies any housing price decline and increases the impact on home-owners' equity? There is a counterparty to that debt that suffers as well. We cannot forget the banks, Fannie Mae, Freddie Mac, and the other institutional holders of all the mortgage paper we have created. Because banks, as we have seen, have become so aggressive in their mortgage lending, much of this mortgage paper will be fairly worth-less when home prices decline, at least as a tradeable financing in-strument. Its new value will be whatever a bank can realize from a quick sale of the house in foreclosure. But if a mortgage is written on 90 percent of the value of a house, and the home price declines 30 percent, the bank will be lucky to recoup half of its invested funds through foreclosure and a forced property sale.

Fannie Mae and Freddie Mac are leveraged over 100 to 1 in ag-gregate (that is, their real assets only cover 1 percent of their loans), so if only 2 percent of their portfolio experienced 50 percent credit losses, they would be technically out of business. The taxpayers would have to pick up the bill under their implied guarantees, a tab that could easily run as much as 20 percent of their total assets, or approximately $500 billion.

And because 40 percent of the total assets of commercial banks are residential mortgages and real estate holdings, a decline of only 12 percent in the price of their entire portfolios of mortgages and owned real estate assets would wipe out their total bank equity, which is typically about 5 percent of their total assets.

Worse, banks don't actually have to lose money before the real threat is realized. The real threat is the loss of confidence of depos-itors in the banking system. If depositors believe there is a chance that their deposits will be impaired, they can withdraw them. Of course, because banks leverage deposits, they have only about 5 per-cent in cash on hand at any time to repay all the depositors. The rest is in illiquid longer-term assets like mortgages and business loans.

If people decide they want to withdraw their money from the bank all at one time, a bank run can start. The federal government has adequate means to prevent a bank run on any one institution, but it does not have the liquidity to save all the banks. Because this would be the first national housing crash, and because almost all banks hold a significant amount of their assets in mortgages, the federal government would have great difficulty guaranteeing all the depositors' funds. We are talking trillions of dollars in deposits that might want to walk out the door in any one day. Even the U.S. government could not borrow that sum quickly, especially when a bank-run rumor was widespread.

A $5 trillion decline in the value of residential real estate in America, or a worldwide housing price decline of $15 trillion, is almost impossible to handle and maintain the stability of the banking system. Very few governments are large enough or have adequate reserves to handle these numbers. The entire GDP of the United States is only $11 trillion, and the entire GDP of all the advanced countries of the world is just $30 trillion. As we saw in the Great Depression, when the world loses its confidence in business and government's ability to properly regulate it, the results can be tragic. It took almost thirteen years for the United States to fully recover from the crash of 1929. Free market economies require the confidence of consumers, workers, producers, lenders, and savers that contracts will be honored and banking and monetary systems will be stable. When we lose the ability of our government to properly regulate free enterprise we run the risk of losing our country and our freedom.

11

Are You in Trouble?

Academic theory and logical explanations for the bubble in home prices are all well and good, but it is homeowners and real estate investors who have most likely purchased this book, and you are very much interested in the bottom line. And that is: Where are home prices going to be in five to seven years, and what actions should you take to protect yourself, your home, and your family?

The following chart shows just how much home prices can decline in real terms just to get them back to their 1997 levels, before most of this nonsense started. The 1997 prices have been adjusted at the general inflation rate so they are now reported in constant 2005 dollars.

Table 11.1 Prediction of Possible Average Home Price Declines by City Over the Next Five to Seven Years

Metropolitan Area	2005 Price	1997 Price (in 2005 dollars)	Real Price Decline Required to Return to 1997 Price Level
Santa Barbara—Santa Maria—Lompoc, CA	$671,247	$271,157	59.6%
San Diego, CA	$567,427	$234,373	58.7%
Salinas, CA	$635,057	$262,382	58.7%
San Luis Obispo—Atascadero—Paso Robles, CA	$578,704	$255,992	55.8%
Orange County, CA	$618,165	$275,518	55.4%
Vallejo—Fairfield—Napa, CA	$468,382	$212,182	54.7%
Ventura, CA	$583,517	$267,198	54.2%
Riverside—San Bernardino, CA	$320,131	$147,460	53.9%
Oakland, CA	$584,355	$270,936	53.6%
Santa Rosa, CA	$573,493	$268,914	53.1%
Los Angeles—Long Beach, CA	$483,330	$227,258	53.0%
Stockton—Lodi, CA	$346,690	$164,471	52.6%
Sacramento—Yolo, CA	$389,134	$184,771	52.5%
Santa Cruz—Watsonville, CA	$725,482	$347,116	52.2%
Nassau—Suffolk, NY	$466,219	$226,278	51.5%
Modesto, CA	$316,576	$154,448	51.2%
San Francisco, CA	$818,252	$409,369	50.0%
Boston, MA—NH PMSA	$455,584	$230,721	49.4%
San Jose, CA	$708,341	$366,897	48.2%
West Palm Beach—Boca Raton, FL	$285,286	$149,396	47.6%
Providence—Fall River—Warwick, RI—MA	$278,377	$147,254	47.1%
Fresno, CA	$244,386	$132,033	46.0%
Sarasota—Bradenton, FL	$233,694	$127,706	45.4%
Miami—Fort Lauderdale, FL	$253,344	$139,843	44.8%
New York—Northern New Jersey, NY—NJ	$454,522	$252,028	44.6%
Worcester, MA	$278,954	$155,277	44.3%
Melbourne—Titusville—Palm Bay, FL	$198,942	$111,017	44.2%
Bakersfield, CA	$183,648	$104,872	42.9%
Fort Myers—Cape Coral, FL	$213,479	$124,177	41.8%

(continued)

Metropolitan Area	2005 Price	1997 Price (in 2005 dollars)	Real Price Decline Required to Return to 1997 Price Level
Newark, NJ	$396,216	$233,782	41.0%
Tampa—St. Petersburg—Clearwater, FL	$176,415	$104,516	40.8%
Daytona Beach, FL	$172,896	$102,939	40.5%
Bridgeport, CT	$349,386	$208,936	40.2%
Reno, NV	$303,073	$185,968	38.6%
Charleston—North Charleston, SC	$170,899	$105,441	38.3%
Trenton, NJ	$252,090	$155,837	38.2%
New Haven—Meriden, CT	$271,943	$172,394	36.6%
Jacksonville, FL	$162,177	$103,295	36.3%
Orlando, FL	$186,297	$122,049	34.5%
Visalia—Tulare—Porterville, CA	$176,690	$116,057	34.3%
Springfield, MA	$191,589	$126,594	33.9%
Hartford, CT	$233,162	$161,084	30.9%
Savannah, GA	$162,935	$114,279	29.9%
Pensacola, FL	$131,186	$ 94,088	28.3%
Chicago—Gary—Kenosha, IL—IN	$255,167	$185,616	27.3%
Tucson, AZ	$175,119	$127,512	27.2%
Tallahassee, FL	$160,585	$116,971	27.2%
Lakeland—Winter Haven, FL	$119,632	$ 87,656	26.7%
Honolulu, HI	$499,612	$368,156	26.3%
Richmond—Petersburg, VA	$167,751	$123,682	26.3%
Albany—Schenectady—Troy, NY	$159,438	$117,824	26.1%
Detroit—Ann Arbor—Flint, MI	$173,547	$131,101	24.5%
Allentown—Bethlehem—Easton, PA	$167,026	$126,823	24.1%
St. Louis, MO—IL	$147,548	$112,228	23.9%
Madison, WI	$210,943	$162,674	22.9%
Anchorage, AK	$238,663	$185,665	22.2%
Atlanta, GA	$180,454	$140,483	22.2%
Kansas City, MO—KS	$142,948	$111,391	22.1%
Lansing—East Lansing, MI	$152,452	$119,834	21.4%
New Orleans, LA	$139,776	$110,177	21.2%
Colorado Springs, CO	$205,975	$164,858	20.0%

Metropolitan Area	2005 Price	1997 Price (in 2005 dollars)	Real Price Decline Required to Return to 1997 Price Level
Fayetteville—Springdale—Rogers, AR	$134,672	$110,097	18.2%
Grand Rapids—Muskegon—Holland, MI	$146,725	$120,239	18.1%
Lexington, KY	$140,959	$115,812	17.8%
Austin—San Marcos, TX	$162,412	$133,633	17.7%
Biloxi—Gulfport—Pascagoula, MS	$109,644	$ 90,405	17.5%
Eugene—Springfield, OR	$184,070	$152,489	17.2%
Saginaw—Bay City—Midland, MI	$113,085	$ 94,410	16.5%
York, PA	$150,864	$126,493	16.2%
Davenport—Moline—Rock Island, IA—IL	$101,475	$ 85,083	16.2%
Binghamton, NY	$ 90,145	$ 75,666	16.1%
Toledo, OH	$129,597	$108,781	16.1%
Reading, PA	$145,034	$121,763	16.0%
Birmingham, AL	$128,932	$108,599	15.8%
Des Moines, IA	$138,465	$116,693	15.7%
Kalamazoo—Battle Creek, MI	$133,648	$112,654	15.7%
Pittsburgh, PA	$107,583	$ 90,792	15.6%
Lancaster, PA	$158,033	$133,595	15.5%
Utica—Rome, NY	$ 93,461	$ 79,067	15.4%
Columbia, SC	$126,444	$106,993	15.4%
Dallas—Fort Worth, TX	$133,725	$113,408	15.2%
Appleton—Oshkosh—Neenah, WI	$137,378	$116,899	14.9%
Syracuse, NY	$101,537	$ 86,460	14.8%
Oklahoma City, OK	$101,829	$ 86,921	14.6%
Tulsa, OK	$107,322	$ 91,717	14.5%
Shreveport—Bossier City, LA	$ 95,092	$ 81,429	14.4%
Knoxville, TN	$131,618	$112,851	14.3%
Corpus Christi, TX	$ 90,000	$ 77,242	14.2%
Hickory—Morganton—Lenoir, NC	$119,555	$103,783	13.2%
Boise City, ID	$146,574	$127,477	13.0%
Lafayette, LA	$106,741	$ 92,977	12.9%
Baton Rouge, LA	$124,275	$109,088	12.2%
Nashville, TN	$159,099	$139,674	12.2%

(continued)

Metropolitan Area	2005 Price	1997 Price (in 2005 dollars)	Real Price Decline Required to Return to 1997 Price Level
Lincoln, NE	$140,766	$123,949	11.9%
Lubbock, TX	$ 94,754	$ 83,433	11.9%
Canton—Massillon, OH	$116,946	$103,036	11.9%
Harrisburg—Lebanon—Carlisle, PA	$141,563	$125,012	11.7%
Peoria—Pekin, IL	$111,774	$ 98,787	11.6%
South Bend, IN	$109,824	$ 97,250	11.4%
Johnson City—Kingsport—Bristol, TN—VA	$103,402	$ 91,715	11.3%
Augusta—Aiken, GA—SC	$106,053	$ 94,162	11.2%
San Antonio, TX	$ 96,445	$ 85,831	11.0%
Jackson, MS	$109,753	$ 97,805	10.9%
Greenville—Spartanburg—Anderson, SC	$118,718	$105,892	10.8%
Little Rock—North Little Rock, AR	$112,268	$100,169	10.8%
Wichita, KS	$103,381	$ 92,307	10.7%
Cleveland—Akron, OH	$145,896	$130,396	10.6%
Beaumont—Port Arthur, TX	$ 77,086	$ 68,917	10.6%
Spokane, WA	$137,949	$123,839	10.2%
Erie, PA	$106,323	$ 95,578	10.1%
Macon, GA	$107,915	$ 97,200	9.9%
Scranton—Wilkes-Barre—Hazleton, PA	$104,430	$ 94,264	9.7%
Rockford, IL	$124,397	$113,242	9.0%
Huntsville, AL	$121,424	$110,608	8.9%
Youngstown—Warren, OH	$ 96,889	$ 88,266	8.9%
Raleigh—Durham—Chapel Hill, NC	$176,273	$161,189	8.6%
Indianapolis, IN	$131,805	$120,533	8.6%
Greensboro—Winston-Salem—High Point, NC	$133,522	$122,220	8.5%
Brownsville—Harlingen—San Benito, TX	$ 71,176	$ 65,456	8.0%
Mobile, AL	$105,904	$ 97,431	8.0%
McAllen—Edinburg—Mission, TX	$ 67,364	$ 62,757	6.8%
Buffalo—Niagara Falls, NY	$108,670	$101,671	6.4%
Killeen—Temple, TX	$ 91,427	$ 85,551	6.4%
Springfield, MO	$110,628	$103,595	6.4%
Dayton—Springfield, OH	$122,264	$114,571	6.3%

Metropolitan Area	2005 Price	1997 Price (in 2005 dollars)	Real Price Decline Required to Return to 1997 Price Level
Salt Lake City—Ogden, UT	$176,857	$166,785	5.7%
Fort Wayne, IN	$103,521	$ 97,650	5.7%
Rochester, NY	$117,972	$112,171	4.9%
El Paso, TX	$ 84,357	$ 80,503	4.6%
Fayetteville, NC	$105,218	$101,090	3.9%
Provo—Orem, UT	$183,121	$177,230	3.2%
Montgomery, AL	$115,889	$112,262	3.1%
		Mean Decline	24.7%
		Median Decline	18.0%
		Top 40 Cities' Decline	47.2%

Source of Analysis: Author

To see how this analysis applies to your own home, you need to estimate what its market value was in 1997. Then multiply this value by 1.212 to convert the 1997 value into 2005 constant dollars and adjust for general inflation. This is the price level your home may return to in more normal times over the next five to seven years. Finally, subtract this 1997 price in 2005 constant dollars from your home's current value, based on an appraisal or recent sale prices of similar homes in your neighborhood. If you divide this difference by the home's current value you can see what the predicted decline in price as a percentage might be.

If you are having trouble finding your particular town in the listing of cities above, then you can use the following quick and dirty first approximation to arrive at what declines to expect to your own property. In general, if your home is worth $100,000 today, expect a 10 percent permanent decline in real value (plus additional temporary declines of 10 to 20 percent if the banking system runs into trouble in the future). If your home is worth $200,000, then assume a 20 percent real permanent decline over five to seven years. If

$300,000, then 30 percent, if $400,000, then 40 percent, and any home worth more than $500,000 today should expect declines of at least 50 percent in the future. For the wealthiest homes to decline by these amounts it will involve not just a readjustment of real estate prices but a new appreciation by the wealthy that buying residential real estate and living in it is not an investment option but pure consumption that has very poor long-term returns associated with it. Additionally, if somehow many Americans and the world's wealthy ever become less self-absorbed and less concerned about their status seeking, one can expect prices in the most exclusive communities to drop even faster. The only force holding up these high prices in these exclusive communities is ego, but to date it has been enormously powerful, even when contrasted with logic, reason, and compassion.

If you are one of the unlucky ones who live in one of the forty-plus cities listed above that are expected to decline by more than 30 percent in real terms, then a great deal more explanation is required.

First of all, basing our analysis on market prices in 1997 allows one to capture the value a market brings to understanding relative values in a community. In essence, I am arguing that market prices have gone a little crazy lately, so why not assume they will return to a more reasonable historical level in the future. A pure free market economist would have trouble objecting to this approach, as it plays off the market dilemma here. The market price is significantly different for these overpriced cities in 1997 than in 2005. They both can not be right, unless underlying fundamentals such as the cost of construction or the length of the coastline has changed dramatically over that time. For reasons discussed below, I choose to believe 1997 was the more rational market value, and I dismiss the market values presented today.

This is a much better approach to predicting declines than the one many other experts take. They often try to create complicated models to arrive at the true inherent value of real estate city by city. While they can make adjustments for such physical differences as average size of the houses and the number of bathrooms, they have a much more difficult time arriving at the value of an amenity such as a spectacular view or a nearby beach. Rather than try to wrestle with regression analyses, I will let the market judge the value to place on these amenities, but I'll use a more rational market price from 1997 that existed before our current problems began.

A typical mistake people make in trying to predict home values is to tie their analysis to average incomes in a particular city. If incomes are twice as high in San Francisco as in Buffalo, they reason that homes should be twice as expensive there. This approach makes two fundamental errors. Home prices in the long run should have little to do with incomes. Just because you make more money does not mean you have to put it into a house. Once you control for the size and the quality of a home, there is little reason that greater incomes should cause home prices to be higher. The reason is that the underlying equalizer in all of this is new construction. If an area with greater incomes were overpaying for homes, builders would recognize the opportunity to profit and just build more new homes.

The second mistake this approach makes is that it does not take into account the vast difference in amenities and land values that can occur across cities. If people pay more to live in San Francisco than Buffalo, it is most likely because they appreciate the amenities more and the underlying land values are much greater. Our approach of going back to 1997 prices captures these differences in amenities and land values, but it captures them at a time when the market was operating more rationally.

Why did I choose 1997 and not some other year? That was the first year when housing prices started accelerating exponentially. There is a clear inflection point in Figure 2.3 around 1997. We do not need to seek possible causes when the price history alone tells us that something funny started happening then. Secondly, Figure 2.3 demonstrated that any unusual price movements relative to the hundred-year norm, such as the boom that started in 1997, typically reverse themselves and return to the norm. This is the premise behind predicting that prices will return to inflated 1997 levels. Historically, they always have returned to normal real levels. As we saw in chapter 1, this is also the exact experience of Japan in the 1990s. The only country that has experienced a full cycle of boom and bust in residential real estate saw its housing prices double in price and then return exactly to where they were prior to the boom.

It was also a good average year for housing. It was not an artificially deflated price year for housing as there had not been a recession since 1991, and it was not overly heated as the peak of the stock market did not occur until 1999 and 2000. Substantial military base closings from earlier in the nineties had worked their way through the real estate markets so that home prices were not abnormally depressed.

Most importantly, 1997 was before most of the problems discussed in this book arose. It was before the Bush tax cut that handed $4 trillion to our wealthiest families, some of which found its way into the real estate market. If such temporary windfalls explain a portion of the increase in home prices in our wealthiest communities, the price increases should not be permanent, as underlying construction costs have not changed.

And 1997 was before the bursting of the dot.com bubble. Again, if home prices are increasing because of people's reluctance to invest in the stock market, the resulting home price increases should be short-lived. A correction in home prices downward will quickly make homeowners realize that their leveraged home equity positions have as much, if not more, risk than their stock portfolios.

While 1997 was before the beginning of the retirement of the baby boomers, if that is what is driving home prices higher, especially for vacation and second homes, then one should expect them to decline in the future. Retirees racing to buy vacation homes today to avoid any possible future price increases are just temporarily pushing up prices until builders can build more homes in those neighborhoods. It is hard to imagine that all the trout streams in the country have been overbuilt to date.

If my thesis is correct, 1997 was a time before most of the banks in the mortgage business went crazy. It predated their use of ARMs and interest-only loans to stretch the amount of money they would lend. It also predated the significant decline in nominal interest rates that has occurred since. One can argue that rate declines since 1981 and increases in lending until 1997 reflected the fact that lending was most likely overly restricted in 1981. But since 1997, lending amounts have skyrocketed, mostly due to the misapplication of a bank qualifying formula that confused nominal rates with real interest rates. By returning to 1997 housing price levels we are returning to a time before banks went crazy with exotic mortgages and the application of an overly aggressive bank qualifying formula.

And 1997 itself was a more normal year for valuing real estate. The GDP was not so highly dependent on housing and housing-related activities. People didn't chase open houses for sale and make multiple offers above the asking price. There was no profound wealth effect or previously booked housing profits due to overvalued real estate, so people were much more rational in their bidding. It was also before the days of refinancings of home mortgages, so there was not a lot of loose cash floating about. Finally, 1997 came before the ensuing boom, so people weren't sitting on big equity positions in their homes that they were anxious to roll over into ever-bigger properties.

Behavioralists will applaud the choice of 1997 as a more normal price environment because it was before the entire boom in prices that distorted the marketplace for pricing. They argue that it was the boom itself that caused prices to trend ever higher as people were caught up in a Ponzi-like atmosphere of ever-increasing profits and potential. After 1997, people became convinced that home prices could only ever go up. Because of this they leveraged their home purchases too highly, they paid too much, and they didn't mind negative carrying costs—they could always recoup them when they sold at a still higher price. They were witness to neighbors and friends cashing out of real estate investments and recognizing abnormally large cash windfalls. Such hard and immediate evidence conflicted with their natural instincts that trees don't grow to the sky, but they let their inductive reasoning dominate their deductive intelligence and chose to believe their eyes rather than their minds. Such is the problem with Ponzi schemes. Evidence of early cash windfalls from an investment runs counter to logic, but when measured in real currency it can be terribly compelling.

How certain am I of these predicted price levels by city? Overall, they reflect what I believe will happen when the housing market adjusts and returns to reality. At the extremes, the experience may differ somewhat. It is doubtful Santa Barbara will see 60 percent real declines in its home values. The reason is that most of its home price appreciation over the last nine years has been in its land values. While more ephemeral than building costs, there does seem to be a huge demand for premium properties on our coasts, and the more prestigious and exclusive the community, the better. Santa Barbara fits this description perfectly.

So Santa Barbara's home prices are being supported by the unusually high underlying land values. People do not pay a huge premium for land in Santa Barbara because it is some kind of ticket to higher incomes. You don't need to live in Santa Barbara to work in Los Angeles. Residents only pay it because they value Santa Barbara's amenities—its weather and its coastline and its views. And I believe they pay a significant status premium because they like Santa Barbara's exclusivity.

Even after the easy bank money departs the system and some rationality returns to the pricing of homes, Santa Barbara will still trade at a significant premium to other homes in the country. But this premium will always be suspect because it will have nothing to do with providing adequate shelter for one's family but rather reflect a culture of consumerism and indulgence and status seeking. People who pay millions to live in Santa Barbara are not investing. It is pure consumption. They are treating themselves to amenities that they and their family can enjoy. And in the case of the artificial status they create by paying so much for simple housing, they had better get great personal satisfaction from it because it is not doing anything productive for the rest of humanity.

At the other end of our predictive price spectrum stands lowly Montgomery, Alabama, which is only predicted to weather a 3 percent real home price decline, on average. For the cities at this end of our spectrum, I would caution that this chart reflects a return to normal times, as might have existed in 1997. As we said in chapter 10, a housing decline in our most overpriced cities will have repercussions across the entire country, causing a retraction in our GDP and a recession, lowering home prices everywhere, and threatening a serious bank run and depression. Obviously, if this is the state of the economy in five to seven years, Montgomery's and other cities' minor predicted declines in home values will be greatly understated. If the entire country goes into a recession, the more modestly priced cities will suffer the greatest number of layoffs, personal bankruptcies, and foreclosures. Therefore, Montgomery, and other modestly priced cities like it will see significantly greater home price declines, more in the line of 30 percent than 3 percent.

A nice test of this prediction is to compare these results with our analysis of how overvalued these cities' real estate markets are relative to underlying rental markets, as we saw in chapter 3. Remember, average housing P/E multiples seemed to have expanded 47 percent or so, inexplicably, given that real interest rates did not change substantially during the period. This ties in quite well with the current analysis, as prices that had appreciated 47 percent too fast would have to decline 32 percent in the future to get back in line with historical average P/E levels.

Similarly, in the rental and home pricing analysis we saw that the most overpriced homes had seen their housing multiples expand from 10 times to nearly 30 times, a 200 percent increase. It would take a 66 percent decline in the future to return these most out-of-line cities back to some reasonable level relative to underlying rents, not that much different from the 60 percent we see in this table of predicted declines.

How can you analyze your personal situation to see if it makes sense to sell now? You should sell any investment or vacation properties that are over $200,000 in value, and for lesser-valued properties, a tough cost-benefit analysis should be run. If your primary residence is worth at least $330,000, and you can sell your home and pocket tax-free profits you should most definitely do it. Real profits or avoided losses should represent at least $100,000 for this size house, and it could mean millions in savings for much higher priced homes. This is real money that will become even more valuable to you as we enter a tight money period associated with a bank pullback. You should do it to have investment moneys to utilize elsewhere, but mostly you should do it to get money out of what is a dead asset, your home. To be happy, you don't need to be investing so much on yourself and your family. Your kids are not going to love you because you have a bedroom they can have when they come home from college. Don't think you have to put the profits in the stock market. If you are interested in status, you can pool your winnings with a couple of friends and open the hottest restaurant in town.

It is much harder for people with $150,000 to $330,000 homes to decide what to do. Because of large transaction costs, I would think that it doesn't make sense for people with homes worth less than $150,000 to do anything but ride out the storm the best they can. Clearly, they will want to get their leverage in order and fix any floaty interest rates on their debts, but selling probably does not net them much in total pickup value. From $150,000 to $330,000, you need to perform an analysis of your total costs, including taxes, and see if it makes sense for you to sell. Unless you are pretty much convinced that a housing crash is coming, you probably won't find it profitable to sell now and buy back later.

Here is a sample hypothetical calculation for a homeowner with a $300,000 home that he owns debt-free. Assume he sells and nets $290,000 after taxes and transaction costs. (This assumes it is his principal residence and he has lived there for at least two years. If it is an investment property, taxes may be avoided by the deduction of other business expenses.) Five years later, after prices decline, he can buy back the same or a similar home for $210,000 plus $6,000 in transaction costs for a total profit of $74,000.

Now if this is an investment property, that is the end of the analysis. The reason is that rental income from the property can be assumed to be equal to annual mortgage, tax, and maintenance expenses. If you have overpaid and this is not the case, then the profits from selling are even greater and must be increased by the net annual amounts you would have had to pay to keep the property over the five years.

Theoretically speaking, this same analysis works for a homeowner who decides to live on the property. By choosing to live in the home, he is deciding to forego rental income, exactly equal to the amounts above, and pay the maintenance costs, so the math is the same as above. The rental income, though, is not actual, but virtual, and approximates the value the owner derives from living in the home. Again, if you have overpaid for the home and your carrying costs are greater than the rental value you enjoy from occupying the property, the profits are even greater and need to be adjusted up by this yearly cost of ownership.

In conclusion, it would be natural for a homeowner to believe that we will never return to 1997 price levels for residential real estate. Even though that is our country's history with real estate prices, and is exactly Japan's experience, it is hard to admit that we might give back all the paper profits we have earned over the last nine years. Surely, the world is different today. On that, you will get no argument. But in meaningful, fundamental ways that impact home prices, namely, in construction costs, average incomes, rental incomes available, and physical layouts like length of coastlines or available views, there has been very little real change over the period. The changes that have occurred—greater emphasis on consumption and status, overly aggressive bank lending, temporary constraints on new building, or buyers' beliefs that prices will always increase in the future—all are really quite temporary in nature. It is the nature of markets that they go up and down. At times they get carried away with short-term and unexpected increases in demand, but they always return to a price level that properly reflects the key fundamentals of price determination.

12

Summary and Conclusions

Is the housing price boom sustainable? This is the ultimate question. If current prices can be justified, then there is much less need to be worried about a possible crash.

If theories that justify current prices are found deficient, then one would expect prices to adjust downward in the future. Even so, it would be nice to have a better understanding of how prices got this high to begin with. If in this book I've shown that there is no reasonable theory that suggests that prices deserve to be at their current highs, and I've made a reasoned argument as to how they got to this level to begin with, I will have gone a long way toward demonstrating that a downward housing price adjustment is imminent.

It's very easy to just dismiss the entire bubble as the result of irrational buyers overpaying for their homes. Such reasoning may indeed be part of the final explanation. But this kind of explanation does not provide us any real insight into how the bubble formed. It is always very easy to dismiss market movements we don't understand as irrational and leave it at that. Unfortunately, by doing so we have not learned anything further about how markets operate and we are left with a lack of confidence in markets in general.

If the real estate market can act irrationally, then what about the stock market? What about the currency market? What about all the goods and services markets in the world? By settling on irrationality as the cause of the current housing boom's high prices we lay the groundwork for a theoretical attack on the very foundations of free market capitalism. If investors, producers, and consumers are not rational in their pricing decisions, then the pricing mechanism fails as a means of efficiently distributing goods and services in a free economy. If we don't learn more about the real causes of the current housing boom we run the risk of losing confidence in the entire free market capitalism system.

So this book has had two purposes. First, to try to debunk theories put forward that supposedly explain the current high prices. And second, to try to explain how prices got to these high levels if indeed they are unsustainable.

Let's see what we've learned so far and where it leaves us. There are many theories in the media as to why housing prices should be high currently, why there is no bubble in prices, and why there is no risk of a price decline in the future. The first such theory relies on arguments of supply and demand to argue that the current economic environment is very strong for housing. Citing the record level of sales, the record high prices paid, and the minimal number of homes available for sale on the market, the housing price bull believes that prices are justified at their current levels and should trend higher. The mistake this bull makes is that he does not realize that such supply and demand characteristics can turn quickly.

Values of goods like houses are driven by underlying fundamentals, the costs of construction, the value of the underlying land, the level of real interest rates, the ease of financing, and alternative rental costs. If these fundamentals change, and they can change quite quickly, the supply and demand characteristics of the market will also change, and very quickly. You don't need to wait to build new houses for the supply of homes for sale to increase. All that has to happen is that existing homeowners decide to put FOR SALE signs in the front yard. This increases the supply of homes for sale immediately. And it is this supply that economics addresses when it talks about the determination of pricing in a market.

Housing bulls often cite the market as the best predictor of future prices. This is normally the case, but in a time when we are arguing that the market price has become distorted, it makes little sense to rely so heavily on market price comparisons. The obvious argument against such logic is to ask such a person which market price he thinks is accurate, today's or the one that was 35 percent lower just five years ago. You can't have it both ways. One of the market prices is wrong. Either the market undervalued real estate five years ago or it is overvaluing it today.

Housing bulls cite demographics as the underlying cause of much of the real estate appreciation that has occurred. They cite baby boomers retiring, but fail to mention their possible downsizing of homes. They mention baby boomers' children buying their first homes, but fail to mention that these baby boomers' parents are dying or departing their homes for assisted care facilities. They mention immigration, but the majority of immigrants in the United States are poor and cannot afford homes, especially those that are appreciating the fastest, those costing more than $300,000. And they mention population increases, but the number of new homes built has far outstripped the growth in the country's population. Sophisticated statistical analyses show no correlation between those states experiencing greater immigration and population growth and higher home prices. Texas, for example, has one of the highest rates of immigration and yet home prices there have appreciated the least of all the major population centers in the country.

Housing bulls also make a number of statements that are just plain wrong. They argue that housing construction costs are escalating, when the opposite is true. They think that larger homes with greater amenities explain the price increases, but statistics shows this not to be the case. The same home sold multiple times over a ten-year period is increasing dramatically in value.

Many housing price advocates believe it is always cheaper to own than to rent, but this is a fallacy. Ownership does bring a tax deduction of mortgage interest, but there is no reason at very high prices that this tax savings will mean owning is always less expensive than renting.

Housing bulls look to the health and growth of the economy as a reason for the increase in home prices. What they fail to see is that the housing bubble is the sole reason there is growth in the economy. Without the housing boom and associated banking, mortgage industry, and construction activity, there would be no economic growth.

Finally, housing bulls point to the homebuilding sector and argue that its healthy profits portend a long and stable housing market. Fundamentally, they fail to understand that homebuilders are sellers, not buyers, of homes. If homebuilders are busy, it could be because they believe the market is overvalued and they don't want to miss the profit opportunity. The high profitability of the homebuilders is the strongest evidence that home prices are truly overvalued. If the high prices were justified by high land costs or restrictive building regulations, then homebuilders should not be able to generate such abnormal profits. The fact that the stock market assigns such a low P/E multiple to the homebuilders suggests that it does not expect the boom in housing prices to continue much longer.

There are two even more popular theories cited for why housing prices deserve to be high today. The first is that interest rates are believed to be lower than normal, and so housing prices should be higher than normal. While often stated as a truism, there is very little real truth in this statement. Most of the decline in interest rates is due to lower inflation, so there has been little change in the level of real interest rates. Even if you believed that real interest rates were lower, you would have to assume that this is because people expect the economy to be weaker. Thus, the growth rate of expected rental income from ownership should also be less, meaning that there would be little real change in the value of properties.

Only if you believe that some supernormal circumstance like the Chinese buying hundreds of billions of dollars of our Treasury securities is artificially driving down real rates of interest would it be reasonable to assume that real rates have declined without a commensurate weakening in our economy. And even if you believe this improbable effect, it does make you wonder how permanent it will be. What will happen to housing prices if the Chinese start selling their Treasury securities and confidence weakens?

The movement of nominal interest rates is a very big part of our story of how home prices got so unrealistically high, but it is not because real interest rates have declined.

The second explanation, popular among academics, for why home prices are high and probably due to stay there is that the supply of new housing construction has been artificially constrained in many of our largest cities and wealthiest communities by local governments. This explanation claims that local governments have inappropriately imposed overly restrictive zoning ordinances and building regulations that get in the way of the building of new homes, which could ease the demand for housing. But as I've shown in chapter 6, they made a fundamental error in their analysis, for what they really uncovered was not massive amounts of raw land suitable for development, but rather a couple of thousand square feet of virtually unusable land surrounding many existing homes. Their methodology asked what extra land was worth in the market, but they forgot to ask how much extra land there was on average. It is as if they were suggesting that the solution to the housing crisis was to build low income housing in the front yard of every mansion in Bel Air. Unfortunately, blaming government regulation and praising the free market is so popular in our universities and in our media today, their reported findings had very broad distribution without anyone asking the fundamental questions necessary to see the weakness in their argument. If people want to blame government for their problems, there will always be academics promoting the free market that will be glad to "prove" their conjectures.

So none of the popular explanations of why housing prices deserve to be at these high levels makes much sense. Before we just dismiss the market as completely irrational, it would help to see if we can better understand how prices got this high. Only then will we be able to judge how sustainable these high prices are.

It turns out that the evidence that prices are unsustainably high is quite strong. First, Robert Shiller has shown that real housing prices after adjusting for inflation and housing characteristics has been relatively flat for the last hundred years. Only in the last nine years have real home prices spiked up by some 60 percent or so. My further analysis showed that real prices have indeed been accelerating, but that their upward movement dates back to 1981, the same year nominal interest rates started their decline worldwide.

A comparison of housing prices to the underlying rental incomes they might earn if leased out showed that they traded in a remarkably tight range until the last five years or so. Not only have housing P/E multiples increased some 47 percent in the last five years, the cities with the highest priced homes have seen their home P/Es explode by 200 percent and more. Any rational explanation as to the cause of the housing bubble is going to have to explain why our wealthiest and most exclusive communities have seen such a divergence between home prices and rents.

The housing market is often characterized as a localized or regional marketplace. Historically, housing prices might be negatively affected in San Francisco and Boston by a high-tech downturn, but the price decline would be limited to these geographic regions and there would be little real national impact.

The current housing boom is not just national, but international. As I showed in chapter 3, with the exception of Tokyo and Frankfurt, the wealthiest cities in the advanced world have seen their real home prices increase anywhere from 30 to 400 percent or more over the last twenty years, with London and New York being the biggest gainers. Again, a rational explanation of what is driving home prices to unsustainable levels must have an international component to it.

The most likely explanation of the housing bubble is the behavior of overly aggressive and poorly regulated commercial banks. As we have seen in chapter 7, those communities that had the greatest access to jumbo mortgages offered by banks and to exotic forms of mortgages such as interest-only loans also experienced the greatest price appreciation. The primary reason the banks caused the current real estate bubble has to do with the way they determine how much money to lend to any particular home purchase. The market for housing may not be completely irrational, but that doesn't mean that the banks are completely rational themselves in determining the amounts to lend.

Banks mostly rely on a qualifying formula in determining how much money to lend to a prospective homebuyer. They then rely on market-driven appraisals of home values to provide comfort that they have not lent too much for a home. But there is a fundamental problem in the bank qualifying formula and how it handles changes in nominal interest rates. As nominal interest rates decline, and real rates remain unchanged, the bank lending formula calls for lavishing ever greater amounts of lending on the potential buyer. This is an error. If real interest rates are not changing, then home buyers shouldn't qualify for higher loans, they shouldn't have more money to bid with, and home values wouldn't be so easily forced up.

This overlending by banks not only explains why the real estate bubble is global—all commercial banks utilize essentially the same qualifying formula—but also why things started to heat up only when nominal interest rates began their decline in 1981. It was a mistake to think that real interest rates were changing over the period, but it wasn't the housing market's mistake or even its fairly rational buyers; it was a mistake in the back rooms of our commercial banks where their lending formulas were calculated. This also explains why home prices diverged from their rental income streams, as only purchases and not leases would be impacted by the banks' communal error.

Of course, it is not enough just to have loose money in a market to cause assets to become overpriced. There still have to be willing buyers who decide the high prices are justifiable and desire to acquire the property at the inflated price. These buyers' task was eased by the fact that up to 100 percent of the purchase prices was being financed by the overly aggressive banks, but the buyer still had to sign what was often a multimillion-dollar mortgage note and, in essence, leverage his future.

In chapter 9 I argued that status seeking is a primary force behind these "willing" buyers. People pay unusually high prices for goods that help them establish premium positions of stature relative to their former peers, and there is no reason they won't use expensive homes and exclusive neighborhoods for the same purpose.

This status-seeking theory seems to fit well with evidence that other status goods like motor yachts and expensive sailboats were appreciating as fast as expensive homes during the last twenty years. Also, such a status-seeker argument fits well with the data that the most exclusive and wealthiest communities have the fastest-appreciating homes. There's no better way to make something exclusive and denote status than to raise its price above the means of average buyers.

Status seeking is not limited to Americans and might also explain the global housing data, especially the dramatic price increases experienced in status centers like Milan, Paris, and London. Finally, status might also explain the divergence of ownership and rental costs, as any true status seeker knows that renting a home in an exclusive neighborhood does not confer the same status and privileges as owning property there.

It is interesting to try to pinpoint exactly which portion of the home purchase has appreciated the most. It appears that housing construction costs have been mostly flat recently, so the increase is either due to higher land values or to restricted supply due to government regulation. I have attacked the government regulation argument, so that leaves the only rational argument for higher home values to be higher underlying land costs. This indeed seems to be the case as those cities that have appreciated the most have very little land still available for development, and raw land in those top cities goes for millions of dollars per acre. It also helps explain the economics of teardowns. It can make good economic sense to buy and tear down a fully functional house if a great percentage of the purchase price is attributed to the land acquisition rather than the cost of the physical structure. And this is just what has happened. Many of the priciest areas for homes in the country have a great number of teardowns and major renovations occurring.

Of course, there still may not be a rational reason for the price increases. Banks erring in how they extend loans explains how we got here, but gives us no confidence that the boom will continue. If they are indeed overlending, either they will return to their senses or there will be enough defaults and foreclosures that they will be forced to change their ways. Either way, these real estate prices will not hold in the future. Similarly, status seeking appears rational in as much as it is a human drive as old as greed, yet the fact that it so unproductive to society as a whole suggests that someday even status seekers will awaken to the fallacy that increased status brings happiness or a full, meaningful life. While it is a "rational" explanation of how housing prices got so high, there is nothing rational about people spending millions on their home while other people suffer from poverty and sickness.

No, a truly irrational argument would have to be along the lines of the behavioralists, who believe buyers are making fundamental mistakes in how they bid for property. While I don't believe that buyers are completely irrational, you can see how the housing market over the last twenty-five years might lead some to fairly irrational conclusions. The strength of the market has led some to believe that prices are almost assured to increase further in the future. Such a belief leads them to pay excessive amounts for homes.

The most damaging aspect of getting caught up in a seemingly ever-increasing market like real estate is the actual evidence of greater profits earned by friends and neighbors. Their profits seem to support a confused logic that says that everyone who participates will always make money. As I showed in chapter 8, this leads to herdlike behavior that is very familiar in Ponzi schemes. Unfortunately, all Ponzi schemes eventually collapse, and the last ones to cash out are those who suffer. Housing is ideal for such gambling because it represents a very large purchase, most of the required funds are financed by a third party, and past profits can be rolled forward into the equity down payments of ever larger and ever more costly homes.

The final argument to convince you that this housing boom is really an unsustainable bubble is that it did not occur by coincidence. It was all very well planned, and great effort is being made to insure it continues. The culprits are our federal government and the regulatory bodies that are supposed to have our best interests at heart. Unfortunately, big campaign contributions and corporate lobbying efforts have shifted the allegiance of our elected representatives from protecting us to worrying about their paying customers— Fannie Mae, Freddie Mac, the big commercial banks, the real estate industry, the homebuilding and mortgage industries.

The reason we are in this mess is that the Federal Reserve decided to lower nominal interest rates to 1 percent to try to avoid a recession after the dot.com bust. This meant that for a period of years they had driven real interest rates negative. This encouraged higher home prices at the same time that people were looking for a safer investment than the stock market.

And Greenspan and the administration have done nothing to deflate the housing bubble since. Greenspan speaks about "froth" in the housing market, but assures people there is no such thing as a national market in real estate. The travesty of course is that all these government agencies have data that clearly show that housing prices take off in metro areas when jumbo and exotic mortgages like interest-only loans are introduced, and yet they do nothing to limit their use. Actually, worse than doing nothing, they meet with commercial banks and homebuilding companies to give them warnings about the unsustainability of high home prices in the market, but refuse to release their comments publicly or give similar warnings to the public.

Government officials hide behind the excuse that the free market will take care of everything if we just allow it to operate. But the housing market is not a free market. There is nothing free market about granting Fannie Mae and Freddie Mac implied guarantees that their debt will be backed by the American taxpayer if there is a problem in the future. There is nothing free market about banks extending trillions of dollars of mortgage loans, taking huge upfront fees, and then selling the assets upstream to Fannie and Freddie. There is nothing free market about buyers bidding for houses with other people's money and no money of their own at risk. There is nothing free market about banks collecting up-front fees on such long-lived assets as home mortgages without any concern for their long-term viability. There is nothing free market about interest rates being depressed temporarily because the world's richest democracy needs to borrow money from the world's largest Communist dictatorship to make ends meet.

As usual, it will be the unsuspecting public that will be left holding the bag when all this gets sorted out. The taxpayer will have to honor Fannie Mae and Freddie Mac debt commitments. The taxpayer will absorb the cost of cleaning up the real estate and mortgage industry. The public will absorb the trillions of dollars of cost of bailing out the commercial banks that get in trouble with their mortgage portfolios. And the public will suffer layoffs and wage hits as they weather the recession or depression that will result when these major housing-related industries plummet, taking the entire economy with them. And during all this pain, the public will wrestle with losing their homes to foreclosure when many will find their mortgage balances far exceed their homes' depressed true market values.

While the highest priced and wealthiest cities of the world are at greatest risk of a correction in home prices, the damage will not stop there. Those most at risk are the people who have stretched their earnings to maximize their leverage and have paid for properties far more than they can afford. But the middle class across the country will also suffer. As foreclosures increase, banks will pull back in their lending, home prices will drop, and the economy will tank. This will lead to layoffs in middle-class towns and more foreclosures and still lower home prices. As is typical, the middle class will suffer the most even though they were not the biggest offenders when it came to paying high prices for homes. A weakened economy will drive all home prices down, and the middle class will suffer the majority of the job layoffs. This will lead to the loss of their homes in many cities that have not participated in the housing boom to date.

America has become a much less democratic, egalitarian, equal-opportunity place to live over the last thirty years. It is almost impossible for an incumbent in Congress to lose a reelection bid given the way congressional districts have been gerrymandered. Presidential candidates of both parties seem to represent the interests of the wealthy and the incorporated who can afford to give them large campaign contributions. Our best private schools are reserved for families that can afford tens of thousands of dollars in tuition while our public schools are in disarray. And for the first time in America, privilege and social position will become inheritable as Congress acts to permanently eliminate the inheritance tax.

America is literally dividing into two countries, wealthy America and poor and middle-class America. Entire communities like San Diego and San Francisco and Manhattan are reserved for the wealthiest. Americans having more moderate incomes are being forced to find homes elsewhere. Low-income Mexican immigration provides a steady stream of cheap labor to our corporations, but destroys our unions and wage structure in the meantime. Globalization puts our poorest in direct competition for jobs and wages with the world's poorest, many of whom live in repressive dictatorships with no guarantee of basic human rights. We are quickly becoming a country of haves and have-nots, with the number of Americans living in poverty increasing for the fourth straight year. The American public never reacted when they watched their precious democracy slowly evaporate before the will of big donors and big business. Now the coming housing crash is the result of allowing our government to work on behalf of our biggest banks and corporations rather than our people. Maybe, just maybe, people will realize that government must be responsive to its people, that free markets cannot operate without proper regulation, and that elected representatives' sole allegiance must be to the people. The people, hopefully, will finally stand up and act to save their republic and assure that the suffering caused by the end of the housing bubble is never allowed to occur on our shores again.

References

Ackman, Dan. March 2, 2005. "Fresh Pricks in the Housing Bubble." *Forbes.*

Becker, Gary S., and Kevin M. Murphy. April 2005. "The Equilibrium Distribution of Income and the Market for Status." *Journal of Political Economy* 113(2), pp. 282–310.

Bergsman, Steve. January 2005. "The Hispanic Housing Boom." *Mortgage Banking* 65(4), pp. 48–54.

Bonner, Raymond. July 5, 2005. "Hole in the Housing Bubble." *New York Times.*

Case, Karl E., and Robert J. Shiller. 2004. "Is There a Real Estate Bubble?" *Brookings Papers on Economic Activity,* 2004-I.

Case, Karl E., and Robert J. Shiller. 1996. "Mortgage Default Risk and Real Estate Prices: The Use of Index-Based Futures and Options in Real Estate." *Journal of Housing Research* 7(2): 243–258.

Case, Karl E., and Robert J. Shiller. 1993. "A Decade of Boom and Bust in Single Family Home Prices: Boston and Los Angeles, 1983–1993." *Revue D'Economie Financière* (December 1993), pp. 389–407. Reprinted in *New England Economic Review* (March/April 1994), pp. 40–51.

Case, Karl E., and Robert J. Shiller. 1989. "The Efficiency of the Market for Single Family Homes." *American Economic Review* 79 (March), 125–137.

Case, Karl E., John M. Quigley, and Robert J. Shiller. 2004. "Home-Buyers, Housing, and the Macroeconomy" in Anthony Richards and Tim Robinson, eds., *Asset Prices and Monetary Policy,* Reserve Bank of Australia, 2004, pp. 149–88.

Case, Karl E., John M. Quigley, and Robert J. Shiller. 2001. "Comparing Wealth Effects: The Stock Market Versus the Housing Market." *Cowles Foundation Discussion Paper* no. 1335.

Clark, Kim. June 6, 2005. "Through the Roof." *U.S. News and World Report* 138 (21), p. 46.

Cooper, James C. November 15, 2004. "Pop Goes the Housing Bubble." *Business Week* p. 36.

Cowley, Geoffrey. June 16, 2003. "Why We Strive For Status." *Newsweek* 141 (24), p. 66.

Coy, Peter. May 23, 2005. "Locating Affordable Luxury Homes." *Business Week Online*. www.businessweek.com.

Coy, Peter. July 19, 2004. "Is a Housing Bubble About to Burst?" *Business Week Online*. www.businessweek.com.

Darlin, Damon. August 13, 2005. "Do Try This at Home: Assess Your Area's Real Estate Bubble." *New York Times*, p. —.

Economist. June 16, 2005. "After the Fall." *Economist*.

Economist. June 16, 2005. "In Come the Waves." *Economist*.

Economist. December 29, 2004. "Faltering Meritocracy in America." *Economist*.

Economist. May 31, 2003. "A Boom Out of Step." *Economist* 367, pp. 5–7.

Economist. March 28, 2002. "Going Through the Roof." *Economist*, p. —.

Fahey, J. Noel. December 2004. "The Pluses and Minuses of Adjustable-Rate Mortgages." *Fannie Mae Papers* vol. 3(4) Fannie Mae.

Fischel, William. 2004. "An Economic History of Zoning and a Cure for Its Exclusionary Effects." *Urban Studies* 41(2): 317–40.

Fox, Justin. June 13, 2005. "Betting Against the House." *Fortune* 151(12), p. 25.

Frank, Robert. December 14, 2004. "Making Waves: New Luxury Goods Set Super-Wealthy Apart from Pack." *Wall Street Journal* (Eastern Edition), p. A-1.

Frank, Robert. 1999. *Luxury Fever: Why Money Fails to Satisfy in an Era of Excess*. New York: Free Press.

Glaeser, Edward, and Joseph Gyourko. 2003. "The Impact of Zoning on Housing Affordability." *Economic Policy Review* 9(2): 21–39.

Glaeser, Edward, Joseph Gyourko, and Raven E. Saks. 2005. "Why Have Housing Prices Gone Up?" *American Economic Review,* forthcoming.

Glaeser, Edward, Joseph Gyourko, and Raven E. Saks. 2005. "Why Is Manhattan So Expensive? Regulation and the Rise in House Prices." *Journal of Law and Economics,* forthcoming.

Glaeser, Edward, Jed Kolko, and Albert Saiz. 2000. "Consumer City." *Harvard Institute of Economic Research*. Working paper.

Glaeser, Edward, and Albert Saiz. 2004. "The Rise of the Skilled City." *Brookings-Wharton Papers on Urban Affairs* 5 (2004): 47–94.

Glaeser, Edward, and J. Shapiro. 2003. "The Benefits of the Home Mortgage Interest Deduction." *Tax Policy and the Economy* 17 (2003): 37–82.

Gyourko, J., and Albert Saiz. May 25, 2005. "Construction Cost and the Supply of Housing Structure." Working paper.

Gyourko J., C. Mayer, and A. Sinai. July 2004. "Superstar Cities." Zell/Lurie Real Estate Center at Wharton. Preliminary working paper, University of Pennsylvania.

Hagerty, James R. June 22, 2005. "S&P, Citing Option ARM's, Sees Growing Risks for Home Loans." *Wall Street Journal* (Eastern Edition), p. A-8.

Hagerty, James R., Dawn Kopecki, and John D. McKinnon. June 15, 2005. "White House Seeks Tougher Bill in Push to Rein in Fannie, Freddie." *Wall Street Journal* (Eastern Edition), p. A-1.

Hagerty, James R., and Ruth Simon. June 20, 2005. "Fannie Sees Higher Odds of Regional Housing Bust." *Wall Street Journal* (Eastern Edition), p. A-8.

Hevesi, Dennis. July 17, 2005. "Which Mortgage? A Complicated Tale." *New York Times*.

"Homebuilders: Get Ready to Raise Roofbeams." August 31, 2004. *Wall Street Journal,* (Eastern Edition), p. A-13.

Ibrahim, S. A. May 2005. "Alarm Over Interest-Only ARM's: Much Ado About Nothing." *Mortgage Banking* 65(8), p. 20.

Ip, Greg. June 20, 2005. "Booming Local Housing Markets Weigh Heavily on Overall Sector." *Wall Street Journal* (Eastern Edition), p. A-1.

Ip, Greg. June 14, 2005. "Crash Test: Does a Housing Bust Hurt More Than a Stock Collapse?" *Wall Street Journal* (Eastern Edition), p. D-2.

Ip, Greg. June 12, 2005. "What Happens If Real Estate Goes Bust?" *Wall Street Journal* (Eastern Edition), p. 1.

Ip, Greg. June 9, 2005. "Side Effects: In Treating U.S. After Bubble, Fed Helped Create New Threats." *Wall Street Journal* (Eastern Edition), p. A-1.

Ip, Greg. October 20, 2004. "Greenspan Again Plays Down Fear of Housing Bubble." *Wall Street Journal* (Eastern Edition), p. A-2.

Jaffe, Chuck. April 8, 2005. "The Risks from Falling Home Prices." *Market Watch from Dow Jones.* www.marketwatch.com.

"Joint Press Release: Agencies Issue Credit Risk Management Guidance for Home Equity Lending." May 16, 2005. Board of Governors of the Federal Reserve System.

Krugman, Paul. August 12, 2005. "Safe as Houses." *New York Times*.

Lahart, Justin. May 24, 2005. "Ahead of the Tape." *Wall Street Journal* (Eastern Edition), p. C-1.

Laing, Jonathan R. June 20, 2005. "The Bubble's New Home." *Barron's*.

Leonhardt, David, and Motoko Rich. June 16, 2005. "The Trillion Dollar Bet." *New York Times*.

Lereah, David. 2005. *Are You Missing the Real Estate Boom? Why Home Values and*

Other Real Estate Investments Will Climb Through the End of the Decade. New York: Currency Books.

Liu, David. 2005. "Interest-Only and Jumbo Mortgage Data." Mortgage Strategy Group, UBS. New York.

Madigan, Keith, Ann Therese Palmer, and Christopher Palmieri. April 11, 2005. "After the Housing Boom." *Business Week,* pp. 78–84.

Mandel, Michael J. June 6, 2005. "The Cost of All Those McMansions." *Business Week,* p. 44.

Manning, Margie. July 10, 2005. "Big Mortgage Portfolios Could Put Banks at Risk." *Tampa Bay Business Journal.*

Maulden, John. July 2, 2005. "Thoughts on the Housing Bubble." *Forex Rate— Currency News.* www.forexrate.co.uk/news.

Modigliani, F., and R. A. Cohn. 1979. "Inflation, Rational Valuation and the Market." *Financial Analysts Journal* 35, pp. 24–44.

Moffett, Sebastian. July 11, 2005. "The Japanese Property Bubble: Can It Happen Here?" *Wall Street Journal* (Eastern Edition).

Molotch, Harvey. 1976. "The City as a Growth Machine." *American Journal of Sociology* 82(2): 309–30.

Mullen, George. June 9, 2005. "The Coming Financial Tsunami." *San Diego Union Tribune.*

New York City Department of City Planning. August 4, 2005. "Booming Beyond Manhattan." *New York Times.*

Poterba, James M. 2000. "Stock Market Wealth and Consumption." *Journal of Economic Perspectives* 14(2).

"Ratios of Home Prices to Rental Prices in Selected Metro Areas." May 27, 2005. *New York Times.*

Saks, Raven E. 2004. "Job Creation and Housing Construction: Constraints on Employment Growth in Metropolitan Areas." Working paper.

Saks, Raven E. 2003. "From New York to Denver: Housing Supply Restrictions Across the United States." Economics Department working paper, Harvard University.

Scherer, Ron. July 15, 2005. "House Not Home: Foreigners Buy Up American Real Estate." *Christian Science Monitor.*

Schroeder, Robert. June 24, 2005. "Housing Markets Show Signs of Bust." *Market Watch from Dow Jones.* www.marketwatch.com.

Shenn, Jody. April 12, 2005. "Amid Housing-Bubble Din, Something Different?" *American Banker* 170(69), pp. 1–3.

Shiller, Robert J. 2005. *Irrational Exuberance,* 2nd ed. New Jersey: Princeton University Press.

Shiller, Robert J. June 2, 2005. "People Are Talking . . ." *Wall Street Journal* (Eastern Edition), p. A-12.

Showley, Roger M. June 15, 2005. "Housing Bubble Blip." *San Diego Union Tribune,*

Simon, Ruth. July 26, 2005. "Mortgage Lenders Loosen Standards." *Wall Street Journal* (Eastern Edition), p. D-1.

Sowell, Thomas. May 26, 2005. "Cross Country: Froth in Frisco or Another Bubble?" *Wall Street Journal* (Eastern Edition), p. A-13.

Statistics Bureau, Ministry of Internal Affairs and Communications. 2005. *Japan Statistical Yearbook.* Table 2.1.

Swibel, Matthew. June 6, 2005. "Retire? Not so Fast." *Forbes* 175(12), p. 100.

Talbott, John R. 2004. *Where America Went Wrong: And How to Regain Her Democratic Ideals.* New York: Financial Times/Prentice Hall.

Talbott, John R. 2003. *The Coming Crash of the Housing Market.* New York: McGraw-Hill.

Timmons, Heather. April 25, 2003. "Shoddy Building in the Housing Boom?" *Business Week Online.* www.businessweek.com/bwdaily/dnflash/apr2003/nf20030425_1874_db035.htm.

Tracy, Joseph, Henry Schneider, and Sewin Chan. April 1999. "Are Stocks Overtaking Real Estate in Household Portfolios?" *Current Issues in Economics and Finance.* Federal Reserve Bank of New York.

Tully, Shawn. April 18, 2005. "The New King of the Real Estate Boom." *Fortune* 151(8), p. 124.

U.S. Bureau of the Census. 2005. *Statistical Abstract of the United States,* 2004–2005. Washington, D.C.: U.S. Government Printing Office.

Veblen, Thorstein. 1934. *The Theory of the Leisure Class: An Economic Study of Institutions.* New York: Modern Library.

Wallace-Wells, Benjamin. April 2004. "There Goes the Neighborhood: Why Home Prices Are About to Plummet and Take the Recovery With Them." *Washington Monthly.*

Wessel, David. May 19, 2005. "Capital: The Fed Starts to Show Concern for Signs of a Bubble in Housing." *Wall Street Journal* (Eastern Edition), p. A-1.

Wolk, Martin. July 11, 2005. "Feds No Longer Dismiss Talk of Housing Bubble." MSNBC. www.msnbc.msn.com.

Index

184 Index